AGAPOLOGY
THE RATIONAL LOVE-PHILOSOPHY
GUIDE OF LIFE

Grateful acknowledgement is made to the following publishers or copyright owners for permission to quote from their publications, which are named in the text: Yale University Press, Harper & Row, Viking Press, Macmillan Company, Charles Scribner's Sons, and Oxford Book Company.

AGAPOLOGY

THE RATIONAL LOVE-PHILOSOPHY
GUIDE OF LIFE

By

WILMON HENRY SHELDON

THE CHRISTOPHER PUBLISHING HOUSE
BOSTON, U.S.A.

TABLE OF CONTENTS

7

PREFACE

Much in this book repeats what the writer said in two previous works: *God and Polarity* (Yale University Press, New Haven, 1954) and *Rational Religion: The Philosophy of Christian Love* (Philosophical Library, New York, 1962). It is the culmination, the climax, to which their arguments lead, going beyond them as it does in what could be a quite novel thesis in the history of philosophy. This novel thesis, which we may fairly call our subtitle, is: *love is one with reason and with chance as properly understood.* Properly understood, we say, because it has not been so until quite recently, as in the work of our physical scientists today—a matter we shall stress anon. And as to our emphasis on polarity in the first of the above named works, we shall see, strange as it may seem at first, that love is the polar union of reason and chance.

But first some remarks about the manner of our investigation, so different from the ways of many, even most of our professed philosophers in Europe and America today. This book certainly claims to be a philosophical work, but not really in the style of these thinkers, who take philosophy to be hardly more than the quest for absolute precision in language, perfect analysis of the meaning of words, concepts, statements, and evidence. They show little or no interest in the character of the real world about us or in us, and still less in the claims of the great religions. We, on the contrary, take philosophy in the original sense of the word: love of wisdom, where wisdom means knowledge of the real world, its make-up, laws, values, *and* what all these may reveal to

9

us human beings as to the goods we crave and the ways to gain them. Philosophy is for us a practical business, where practical means seeking the greatest possible good for all through the road of knowing the maximum possible about reality—hence religion, too, comes within its domain. These analytical thinkers are indeed right in demanding clearness in our thinking and our language, but that demand shouldn't go to their exclusive extreme of coining more and more abstract technical terms which quite blot out any appeal to the deep underlying motives of our human *living*. You may say that this is just what the admired physical scientists are doing, with their terrifically refined and complicated mathematical terms and equations. But the difference there is that the scientists always come back to the real world, with their practical experiments to test the results of their calculations. The analytic philosophers do not. And the distinction between physical science and genuine philosophy lies in what we just said about the latter: it treats also of the goods, the values which we may gain through knowledge, what they are and should be. The scientist has indeed contributed much to our human goods by his discoveries; but that is not the central motive of his work, which is knowledge just for the *single* good, knowledge itself. The analytic philosophers, lacking the experiment-motive which would bring them back to reality, remain in the realm of their highly refined techniques, so complicated and refined as to lose any bearing on the underlying motives of mankind's living, with their search for the ways to the goods of life. Clearness in thinking and language we must have, *yes:* but that clearness must not lose its appeal to practical common sense, which respects those goods. After all, common everyday language *can* be made clear enough for the pursuit of wisdom which is philosophy—as we earnestly hope to show in our writing throughout this book. The philosopher wants, needs, to appeal to his fellow-men through his language, and human language normally conveys and should convey emotions and urges to act, as well as thoughts. Mere clearness of thinking *alone,* which is the occupation of the analytic philosopher with his ingrowing intellectual conscience, can never satisfy the inborn quest of human nature for the wise conduct of life. His work is an abstraction away from reality. Let him abandon this language so highly refined as to lose any appeal to our practical human nature— all this "meta-" business, meta-language, meta-geometry, meta-ethics, and so on, but alas! no *meta*physic—and return to the simple language of everyday words which may so well contain the moving, stirring quality bearing on practical living. That we shall try to do.

And let us here notice that our thoroughly rationalist philosopher, Brand Blanshard, has shown in his book *Reason and Analysis* (Open Court, Lasalle, Illinois, 1962), with its 505 closely printed pages, that reason itself, if they would properly use it in their analytic work, drives these analysts out of their ivory tower into the domain of the real world and a consequent metaphysic. Philosophy is metaphysics or it is nothing! And metaphysics is a guide to right living or it is nothing!

Now for a concluding remark. We spoke of the tremendous complexity of the researches made by the analysts, and of the need for a simple language with its direct bearing on the practical. Well, this simplicity applies also to the arguments, concepts, and principles which we shall set forth. The basic principles of reality, we claim, are utterly simple, self-evident to common sense if we look at them without bias. Doesn't the scientist explain the terrific complexity in the world about us by his *simple* laws: gravitation, electric attraction and repulsion, and so on? Even in the natural world quite apart from our thinking, see how the simple little things give rise to the huge and mighty. The big tree with its enormously complex system of trunk, branches, leaves, blossoms, and fruits comes from the simple little seed. The gigantic force of the long freight train is due to the simple little gaseous elements expanding deep within the engine. And what of the frightful power of the bombs, due to the nuclear fissions within the minute atom? Surely the complex is ever accounted for by the simple, the great by the little. So in the following arguments we shall try to speak in the simple non-technical terms of common language, leading thereby to the revealing of the simplest ultimate principles, truth which "needs but to be seen" to be accepted.

So now to state in briefest form our thesis and to justify our endeavor to prove it.

AGAPOLOGY
The Rational Love-Philosophy Guide of Life

CHAPTER I

TO STATE AND JUSTIFY OUR PROJECT

Note the significance of the one newly coined word in the title of this book. The word *Agapology* is of course derived from the Greek words *agapé,* here understood as the love taught by the Christian religion, and *logos,* reason. So we shall mean by it the *unity* of love and reason. We don't take the ending "ology" to mean *merely* "the science of"—as in biology, the science of life, and in psychology, the science of mind. We do include that meaning, we do claim to study the nature of love in a thoroughly rational way; but we go further and aim to show that this love and reason are two phases of one and the same principle. And we shall go still further to the climax of our argument: reason wedded to love sees that love as taught by Christianity—and other religions too—is the very basis of reality, just because the nature of this love reveals the apriori logical necessity of the being of God, the Perfect One, Who created this universe, loves His creatures and would have His love infuse their being to the utmost. And in reaching this climax we shall see why, strange and wild as it must seem, our subtitle includes its last noun *chance* —that word as we said above properly understood, as it has not been in the past but is seen in a new light by our scientists today. For we shall see that chance, *rightly understood,* shows *why* the nature of love, wholly rational as it is, means what we just said; the apriori logical necessity of God's being as Perfect Love. Yes, we shall find that all three: love, reason, and chance are one!

Why Then Put Love First?

Why then do we choose as the outstanding word of our title *Agapology* which puts *agapé* first, *logos* after it, and doesn't mention chance at all? If these three are really one at bottom, why call our thesis Agapology rather than Rationalism or Tychism? The answer is: because our philosophers and theologians of the past, dwelling too exclusively on reason or faith or revelation, have failed to see that if we study the meaning of love we can discover the solution of mysteries hitherto baffling, especially the central one above noted: *why does God exist?* Love has been too much neglected by reason! And the remarkable point in this investigation of love's meaning is that it enhances our respect for reason in religion—and for chance, too, which has been hardly respected at all— since we find love including both reason and chance. Yes, we choose the new word of our title just because the love-thesis needs an emphasis which has not been given it, fruitful as we shall find it to be for the discovery of new truth. And above all, to respect love is to move into the practical field, the search for the goods of life: philosophy, the guide of life, as we said in the Preface.

But anyway, quite apart from our climax-argument, revering reason as most of us do—witness our high regard for the sciences. And coming as we are, however slowly, to minister lovingly more and more to the needs of our fellow-creatures— witness for instance the new Peace Corps at work today, surely we should be gratified to see that there is no opposition, no separation or gulf between these two revered goods, reason and love. How many of mankind's woes, past and present, have been and are due to the separation, the opposition between them—as in the great religions and their fights, and of late the fairly widespread hostility between science and supernatural religion! Surely also to see and feel this unity of reason and love should lead us as our civilization advances in intelligence toward a peace on earth never yet reached. And all the more so if we come to see with our argument here that love is a principle at the very basis of reality. There lies the justifying of this book. Even should it fail in the endeavor, the motive needs no defense. *No apology for Agapology!*

A Recent Philosophy Not Far From This

It is interesting here, and may throw a more favorable light on our thesis, to take a look at the philosophy of Charles S. Peirce, highly respected today as an eminent thinker. He taught that love is a basic principle of reality. He named this doctrine *Agapasm*. The difference of his title from ours is noteworthy. He did not claim to deduce the love-principle from any apriori demand of reason. Hence the ending "asm" which is shortened from "Agapé-ism" where "ism" means a doctrine, a belief, even to many people a dogma of faith alone, though not that last to this rationalist thinker. Peirce's *Agapasm* was based on empirical evidence drawn from history. Our Agapology agrees with it so far, but would go a step further, doing what he didn't try to do, to show that *agapé* is an apriori logical necessity, a supreme value at the very root of reality.

And there is a second respect in which we are rather near to the teaching of this admired philosopher. He taught also that chance is a fundamental principle of reality; he based this, too, on empirical evidence. We shall do likewise; yet

here as with the love-principle we shall claim that chance is
an apriori necessity—indeed, wild as we said it must seem at
first, that love and reason and chance are but three phases of
one and the same apriori principle. To be sure, he didn't
mean by chance quite what we shall mean, but there is a
common element in both which is significant for our thesis.
See then the resemblance of the metaphysic we shall offer to
that of this recent philosopher, profound rationalist, yet defending love and chance as well. That resemblance by the way
is nicely revealed in the title of a collection of his essays edited
by Morris Cohen: *Chance, Love, and Logic.* As these are his
three principles, so are they ours, save that they are with us
three-in-one—a notable likeness, we may here point out, to
the Christian doctrine of the Trinity which we shall later
emphasize.

A Long-Lived Philosophy Likewise Near

This mention of Christian doctrine brings up another point
which will throw light on the metaphysic we here set forth.
It is, we say, rather near to that of Peirce. Now we add: it is
also close to a system usually considered quite unlike the latter, Thomism. As will appear in the following chapters, we
accept the main positive teaching of that great synthetic philosophy; but with our doctrine of chance we *add* a principle
which could hardly have been respected, even thought of,
when the system was founded by St. Thomas Aquinas. For
this mediaeval rationalist chance would be irrational, it
couldn't explain anything. But in recent years, as we said
above, the proper meaning of chance has come into the light,
a meaning unearthed by our physical scientists which we shall
see to be perfectly rational, and which does not at all conflict
with the Thomist synthesis. True, we shall claim that our
human reason can go further than St. Thomas declared it
could go, and the Thomists today may not accept this claim.

But there is in this claim nothing which denies the positive teaching of the system. We claim only to *add* something thereto. In brief, the metaphysic we here offer resembles in the main these two supposedly far apart philosophies, and we would see their teachings united in harmony, opening the way to mankind's increasing progress in love, knowledge, and active living.

An Objection To Our Project

But now pause a moment—a troubling question comes. We said in the Preface that philosophy is, and should be, a practical business, a proper guide of life. We accused our present-day analysts of turning quite away from that. Well, aren't we about to do the same thing? Surely the task we are setting before us—to prove by strict reasoning the apriori necessity of love as identical with God the Perfect Being—surely this demands a treatise so abstract, abstruse, so utterly remote from the pressing needs of mankind, especially today with our wars, hot and cold, our desperate need of world peace, our increasing crimes, and so on—yes, so utterly remote from these that we are doing nothing whatever of the slightest use for the goods of suffering humanity, just a purely theoretical business with no practical bearing at all.

Yes, this would be so, were it not for the *subject* of our reasoning, our theorizing: love. Love is the center and core of our Christian religion, and we should know all that it means and implies. Indeed, shouldn't a love which respects the practical needs of us all, respect also the needs of our intellect? And the prime need of intellect is to understand *why*. Why then is love the center and core of religion? When we come to understand this, then we shall respect, revere, and *practice* love as we couldn't do otherwise. Yes, our undertaking should strengthen the love-motive, even if it doesn't at once offer some particular immediately useful social plan.

There is another reason for our quest. Even if it gives no results, of *immediate* practical value, it might well have a practical result before very long, centered as it is on religion, on one of the deepest hostilities in human history, persisting as ever today.

Also A Particular Deeply Important Practical Need

Look at the three branches of mankind's search for truth and his claim to have discovered it: science, philosophy, religion. Disagreements within each there have been and still are. The least are found in our physical sciences today with their most conscientious efforts to settle them by empirical evidence. With the philosophers, the conflicts between their systems are greater. The reason needn't concern us now, the simple fact is that the philosopher tends to love a certain system, tends rather to refute the other systems than to see what truth they may contain. True, there is in him to some degree a respect for reason which has sometimes opened the gate to an endeavor to harmonize the conflicting systems, even though the endeavor hasn't yet gone very far in convincing his fellow-thinkers. But sharpest of all has been the disagreement between the religions, the theologies. And this is surely due to the central motive of religion with its eager quest for the maximum *good,* that good so deeply appealing to *emotion* as well-nigh to rule out the demand for rational evidence. After all, *emotion* is *motive, moving,* the basic moving force in our human lives. Even the search for knowledge as in the sciences is due to the *craving* for knowledge. So then the group to whom one set of goods appeals most will hardly agree with the group to whom a different set of goods appeals most. Witness the conflict between the Buddha's teaching of Nirvana and Christianity with its "social gospel". And as these goods are for each group the absolutely demanded goods for *salvation,* without which—at least for some groups—will come the torments of *damnation,* each religion can hardly avoid seeing the others as not only mistaken, but *bad.* They are heresies and must be suppressed to save mankind! Whence have come persecution, martyrdom. The scientists, guided by the single emotion alone, love of knowledge based on empirical evidence, will all alike follow where that evidence leads—no fighting between them, no persecutions. And the philosophers likewise, if to a lesser degree, since there is with them more of the emotional factor—for example, the *appeal* of logical elegance with the rationalist at one extreme, the *appeal* of feeling, faith, the deciding will, with the existentialist at the other extreme. Yet the respect for evidence by reason tempers the philosopher's quest; even the existentialist would persuade by argument. For that matter, the earnest religious one would do the like, would try to persuade by argument—but if his opponent refuses to be convinced, suffering, even damnation must be his lot. One's own religion *alone* is right, the one road to perfect bliss!

Yet most if not all of mankind's outstanding religions have proclaimed the love-motive, even if some more than others. And what does this motive imply? Certainly it implies respect for our deep human needs—intelligence is one of these. Should we not then seek to understand the appeals of the different goods declared by the religions? Why does the goal *Nirvana* appeal to the Buddhist? Is there not *something* positive in the experience which our Christian teaching can accept without excluding the joys of daily living as that goal has done? Recall the words used by Christians: "the peace of God which passeth understanding." And what of Islam's doctrine of the duty to welcome all races alike as our brothers and sisters? Christians haven't all been treating the Negro race as fairly as the Moslems have done. And isn't there a fighting trend even within our Christian body, a trend hardly present in the Eastern religions, more tolerant as they are? No other religion has as many disagreeing sects as the Protestants have, with their more than 250 different sects. True indeed, they are today more sensitive to these conflicts and are trying to overcome them with the World Council of Churches. Notice, too, the recent declarations of the Popes, John and Paul, in this direction. Yes, the love-motive is so far increasing; but why stop at the boundary of the present Christian theologies? Why not carry this motive beyond, applying it to all religions, to see if they have truths and values which we can add to those we already have? But to do this is to discern impartially, with no bias beforehand, the logical implications of their doctrines, whether they are consistent or not with the principle of universal love. As we just said, movement in this direction has of late begun as applied within the Christian fold —our own Christian love-motive demands its extension more and more. Yes, if we can understand *why* these different sets of goods appeal to their disciples, we can see whether or not they agree with that motive and so far as they do we shall include them in our religion, thereby removing the iron obstacles to the cause of peace between the fighting creeds. Emotion needs reason! And we may note here another move in this direction, the latest book by the highly respected theologian, Paul Tillich, *Christianity and the Encounter of the World Religions,* Columbia University Press, New York, 1963.

Indeed, we may go further and see a practical result of this love-motive in religion in the sphere of world politics. Of course you would naturally say that settling the religious quarrels has no bearing at all on our so prominent trouble today, the fight between Communism and Democracy. That is a fight in the arena of economics and politics. What has a supernatural religion with its concern over salvation in heaven to do with these?

Also In The Political-Social Fights

Well, if your religion is filled with the love-urge, it will be concerned with all manner of possible goods; not just those of a future life in heaven, but those of your earthly life, those which a proper economics and politics would help to secure. And the communists and capitalists did honestly believe, each of them, that their own scheme would promote the richest, happiest life for us all here and now. What these social plans are based on is really the love-motive, however limited or mistakenly applied. That motive would, if rightly acted on, do away with all such quarrels by asking if there is not *some* possible good in each of the plans. Let the communist try his proposed way of life *in his own group,* to see if it does succeed. Let the capitalist do likewise—*neither interfering with the other.* This is the experimental rational scientific method. No social scheme can prove its rightness beforehand by *mere* reasoning, no scientific theory can prove its truth without verification by experiment. That experimental way is the truly rational way, the way demanded by the *practical* love-motive. And surely the claim we are making in regard to mankind's religious fights—to try to see what goods each has succeeded in delivering and could deliver—is just what would *strengthen* the like behavior in regard to the economic-political fights. No, there should be no separation, no gap between religion and the goods of daily earthly living, the proper social schemes. Love demands that!

Notice, too, that of late, the Russian communist has more of this peaceful experimental attitude than in former years. Witness the recent test-ban agrement. Aren't we coming, even through the negative motive of fear of destruction by the terrific bombs, to *feel* the value, the desperate need, of peaceful coexistence on earth? Let our religions not only cease fighting but concentrate more on the goods of the flesh *as well as* the spirit.

No Final Separation Of Church And State

Let the good Christian remember that the beloved Founder of his religion was concerned not only about man's future life in heaven but showed in His active daily living a care for the goods of earthly life here and now. He healed the sick, gave food to the multitude, comforted little children, reformed the harlot. It has been said that His teaching wasn't good enough because He didn't set forth any economic or political scheme —He said nothing about the proper form of government, the State. Why didn't He? Because He went beneath all that to the fundamental basis of all good living, social and individual alike—the love-motive. Cultivate that, live it, *think* what it implies, experiment with it in good scientific method! If we have the genuine love-motive, He knew that we will come, however slowly and through many mistakes, to see the proper ways in our social and individual behavior. And many of our Christians today are coming to realize this, in what they call the "social gospel". So, too, the "humanists" of today, though they go to the other extreme and deny the supernatural. Yes, the separation between Church and State, so prominent to-day, must *some day* be abolished, even if we are not quite advanced enough for that today. After all, it has been largely due to the too exclusive emphasis of our religion on the goods of life in heaven and the ways of gaining them by our behaviour as individuals on earth. Away with all this exclusion! Love welcomes all possible goods of whatever sort, so long as they don't conflict with one another.

An Objection From Science

Such is our answer to the above objection which pointed to the distracting problems of our public life today, as quite remote from our present project. But now there confronts us another and more positive objection to our proposal, and likely to be made by the empirical scientist whose reasoned evidence we highly respect. To one who looks at the results given by the physical sciences today, especially by astronomy, our thesis appears petty indeed. What is this love that we are exalting to high heaven, just a human feeling, no more? How utterly absurd to think that a feeling in the mind of tiny man on this little planet could have any bearing at all on the universe of the incredibly vast and mighty galaxies! Even in the arena of our human life, so small as compared with the earth whereon it lives, it is surely ridiculous to think such a personal emotion capable of throwing light on the long ages of biological evolution, of human history, with mankind's frightful cruelties, ignorance, pains and death. And what of the beasts and plants, the oceans, deserts, mountains, what of the earth's geological history with its recurring ice ages? Yes, it does look as if there was never so obvious a case of wishful thinking, man trying to make vast and mighty reality in his own tiny image, and only one small part of his image at that—just his little emotion of love. Yes, if it is absurd in respect to his earthly planet, how much more so is it when we consider, as just mentioned, the gigantic universe beyond. Read *Stars and Galaxies* (Thornton Page, ed., Prentice-Hall, Englewood Cliffs, New Jersey, 1962) and you will be so overwhelmed by the spectacle of this universe that the undertaking we are to make seems like a baby alone in the wilderness crying for its food! See, too, how this applies to man's religions—what have the alleged gods, the one God, to do with the many frightfully huge "island universes", receding into empty space at a speed far beyond human sensing, describable only by abstract mathematical symbols? All these religions are only man-centered, all a matter of the hopes and fears of this little human animal struggling for his own petty happiness, nothing whatever to do with these giant beings, powerful beyond his comprehension, utterly indifferent to the needs man wants satisfied—and wanting that, somehow conjures up a Being who will satisfy them. Yes, our religions—and most of our philosophies, too—have just viewed the vast incredible extent of reality as centered around tiny little mankind! And perhaps there are other conscious beings in some other planets in our solar system or in other solar systems. Why not center reality about them too? Could their philosophies agree with ours?

Yet there is an answer. Even though all this is the case, our human quest is justified if it really does meet our human needs. After all, we are just as *real* as all these universes together. And we have our *values, goods.* Where are the goods in these physical galaxies? We are so awestruck by their size, their *quantity,* that we overlook that phase of reality, *value,* which however tiny is just as real as the greatest possible quantity of physical being. The great doesn't exclude the little! Above all, isn't consciousness something higher, more worthy of *respect,* than any amount of physical being? To be sure, the materialist claims that consciousness is only a certain combination of minute physical trends, as in little man's brain and nervous system. Yet it has *values,* not present in the inorganic realm, and even the materialist feels that they *ought* to be realized. Certainly we have the right to ask if there may be a principle of perfect *good* available for our needs—no matter what the size and power of this universe. But of course we must give evidence of such a principle.

And the like holds with respect to the conscious minds—if there are any—on other planets in the great universe. They, too, have their right to center the universe on their goods, whatever those may be. That doesn't make our human viewpoint wrong; nor theirs either! It might even be the case that this mighty universe is governed by principles, laws, which our little intellects may discover—which principles might point to an underlying love-principle at the heart of all being. Anyway, does size make any difference in nature's laws? Witness the discoveries made by the scientists in the ultramicroscopic realm, the laws of electric attraction, radiation, and such, which do apply to the behavior of nebulas, stars, star-clouds. And the laws of gravitation which hold of events on our tiny earth, apply also to the movements of these giants. But above all, there is one principle, simplest of all, not in the least a matter of quantity, which commends itself at once to the reflecting intellect as an apriori universal rule: for everything that is, no matter how big or little, good or bad, there is always a *reason why*. And if, when we see the implications of this apriori necessary principle, as we shall do in the argument to come, if then we find that it implies the apriori necessary existence of a Perfect Being, even apart from His being the Creator of this universe, this conclusion stands on its own feet, quite independent of the matter of gigantic quantity. God is not a quantity! He is no "Big Man in the Sky" to use the telling phrase of George Perrigo Conger. He is not so many trillions of cubic miles wide and deep, so many quadrillions of years old. No, our argument to come is indifferent to the size of this universe, it holds whatever that size, whatever its age. And it is also true whatever be the viewpoints of any other minds on any other planets. Reason holds everywhere!

So—to return to the claim of our thesis—we shall begin by witnessing a principle seeming to be at work in our little human arena of values, goods. And it will turn out to be an essential principle of all reality—the principle named by the last noun in our subtitle, *chance*.

Well now, in virtue of what we said about it—recall the words "strange and wild as it seems"—it surely behooves us to make clear what it means when "properly understood". Certainly the notion of chance as something ultimate, essential to reality, must seem revolting to the rationalist—and we have claimed to be rationalist. So then let us state the meaning of this term.

What Chance Means

It has been brought out recently by the physical scientists in their principle of statistical law. A statistical law permits variations within certain limits which it dictates, and finds that all these possible variations occur about equally in the long run. Each particular variation within those limits is a matter of chance, not determined then and there by the law itself. What is new in the principle is that *all possible variations* are realized sooner or later and *with no preference of some over others,* hence equally within the limits prescribed by the law. So now chance means *the realization of all possibles,* no one instance determined by any other instance, and law is but the *restriction* of the possibles within certain limits. Chance is more positive than law! And this note of chance does seem to be pretty well verified by our scientists; all the known laws of nature seem to be statistical. But we now only point out the positive character of chance as the trend to realize all possibles equally, no conflicts between them, no exclusion of one by another. Later we are to argue that this is a *wholly* rational affair, an apriori necessity. At any rate it isn't so negative, so empty a conception as the rationalist has deemed it in the past.

But now you ask: what has this to do with love, center of our attention here? Cold, impersonal, abstract as this principle of chance appears to be, what possible relation can it have to that warm moving power which is love? We answer: if you study carefully the meaning, the nature of love, a certain likeness between these two "swims into your ken". Has anyone analyzed thoroughly that nature? Love has perhaps been written about more than any other human trait—

in love-stories, dramas, in the biology and psychology of sex, yes even in treatises on religion which take it as an attribute of God far, far above our limited comprehension—yet with little analysis of its content. The great religions, especially Christianity, have proclaimed it as a high virtue, usually taken for granted in the latter as a divine grace needing no analysis, even defying analysis. St. Paul's adoration of love in the Epistle to the Corinthians does state its noble traits, but gives no reason for its being and its creative power. To be sure, some noted philosophers have stressed its central value for life—Plato, Augustine, Aquinas, and in our own day, Erich Fromm, Rufus Jonas, Royce, Hocking, Urban, and Peirce as noted above. Yet these profound thinkers haven't quite explained the underlying trait which makes love a basic reality, a power at the very root of being.

Hear then our thesis, wild as it still must seem, not only to our analytic thinkers today, but also to our rationalist metaphysicians—just because it unites love and chance. Reason seeks to answer the question: why anything is what it is. Well, our argument will claim to show that love is *its own reason for being real*. God is self-existent because God is love. All this because the definition of love will be seen to have the same meaning as the definition of chance we gave above. Love is, we shall see, the realizing of all the positive potentialities, possibles, in the beloved object. Chance is the realizing of all possibles. Isn't the likeness of the two striking? But further, as we said above, we shall argue that this principle, which is the same in both, is an apriori logical necessity, shown by reason itself—hence the unity of chance, love and logic. Yet the importance of this result would not be discerned if we didn't approach it through the meaning of love, center and focus of the love-religion Christianity, and present in other religions. The love-religion came first, if you please, as a revelation; the time is now ripe to see it as a wholly rational necessity, and a necessity quite in accord with the methods and results of the devotee of science. Yes, the love-approach to a metaphysic brings to light the very ground of being and goodness. Such is the Agapology here to be presented.

In fact, as we look over the long history of mankind, this emergence of our Agapology doesn't seem quite so strange. Rather, it seems just the thing natural to the present stage of this history. Roughly speaking, there are three great stages thereof, stages overlapping of course, yet differing as they stress mainly in turn one of the three deepest of man's cherished goods. First and longest of all came the worship of power, power of the gods, kings, mighty heroes, of one's own clan, nation, and of one's self—hence the agelong fights between groups, nations, and individuals. Only the strongest will survive! Then, late on the scene, came the worship of knowledge, of intellect as man's best gift, beginning largely with the Greeks and growing to its widest spread so far in our high respect for science today. No longer is it the strongest who survive; man has survived and progressed—so we are told —because of his intelligence. True, there is an overlapping here. It was Francis Bacon in the late middle ages who justified knowledge in his statement "knowledge is power". And indeed we feel the like today—witness our powerful machines made possible by advances in scientific discovery. But *also* we do cultivate knowledge as a good just in itself.

And now, with our dread of terribly destructive wars, we long for peace, for worldwide friendly cooperation as never in the past. The strong nations are helping the weak as never before. Even if this is to a degree for their own interests, the strong nations in the past fostered their interests by fighting to conquer rather than by gestures of helping. Also our charities today far surpass anything in the past. The love-motive has emerged as never before, and in public affairs too. Especially is this the case in the strong and wealthy U.S.A. See the evidence in the following statement from the *United States News and World Report* of June 17, 1963, headed "Americans Set a Record for Giving". To quote: "Americans gave an estimated 9.3 billion dollars to public causes in 1962 —an all-time record for philanthropy. The American Association of Fund-Raising Counsel, Inc. said individuals contributed the largest share—7.4 billion dollars. Foundations gave 700 million, business 470 million, and 700 million came from charitable bequests. Religion was the biggest beneficiary with 51 percent of the gift total." Isn't it significant that so large, strong and wealthy a nation is so deeply imbued with the love-motive? Plainly we are entering the third stage, however slowly the world over, a growing recognition of the love-urge as fundamental for mankind's welfare. Someday *mankind* will mean *kind man!*

In fact, we shall later give empirical evidence that as regards this matter of the three stages there is a general law at work, what we shall name the *Law of the Three Stages*. It is a law whose presence and deep significance for the future of humanity has not, so far as we know, been noticed at all. It is, we shall see, the temporal expression of the three principles: chance, logic, love. Even more, it is the temporal analogue of the Divine Trinity. It is, we shall stress, a basic *law* of progress which cannot but be fulfilled in time.

Well then, Agapology is the philosophy natural and proper to this now entering third stage. And the unique point here is that, unlike the early worship of power which worked *against* the love-motive, unlike the worship of knowledge which has been in the past rather *indifferent* to that motive, the third stage gives ways to *both* power and knowledge in gaining the goods of life. Love, we shall stress again and again, is not love without both knowledge and power shown in loving deeds. It is the all-inclusive good. It is the key to the fuller

understanding of reality and to the application of that understanding as the one way to the maximum good for each and
for all here and hereafter.

But now let us end all this talk about whether our undertaking is desirable or possible or useless or impossible, and
heed our own stress on the practical: go to it, do it!

Love is a good thing, most of us will agree. Let us then begin by seeing that what is good has a certain power of its
own to realize itself. That will lead us step by step to see that
in the end value, the good, is one with being, love the supreme
good, love the principle of self-realization—all because
chance, love, and logic are at bottom one and the same.
Notice, too, that what we are to set forth in the next chapter
is a wholly empirical matter—no appeal as yet to any apriori
principle. And it is centered on a very limited region—the
little arena of living beings on this tiny planet. Yet, however
limited, however occupied with merely empirical observation,
it will bring to light a principle which is at the very root of
reality, an apriori necessity in itself, and a very simple principle, as we stressed above, indeed the simplest of all.

See then the empirical evidence for the good as self-
realizing.

CHAPTER II

THE GOOD IS SELF-REALIZING

Note first of all that good can be present only where there are conscious minds. Mere physical being isn't just by itself either good or bad. The beautiful sunset as a merely physical event is just a procession of light-rays; it must be presented to a spectator, a conscious mind, to have its beauty *realized*. Beauty is, if you please, *latent* there, it is so far a *source* of beauty, when those minds come on the scene. And the like holds when we have a bodily pain. As just a physical fact in your body it is certain conflicting trends in the processes going on there; but *merely* conflicting trends aren't bad, painful unless felt so—there is nothing bad so far when a falling meteor hits a rock and smashes it. So our study here is concerned with what goes on in conscious minds, and naturally in the most highly developed conscious minds, those of us human beings. Hear then our thesis.

For us human beings, whatever is *felt* to be good has by its very goodness an urge, a force however slight, acting on the one who feels it, to realize it. So it has to that degree a power to make itself exist—if nothing interferes. Recall the saying: "the good is its own excuse for being." It may happen to be an actually existing good here and now, as when we are listening to beautiful music. In that case we feel the urge to continue its being. What we enjoy we don't want to have interrupted, we would continue the experience as long as we can, as long as it can be a joy, until it palls on us. As wrote the deeply philosophic poet Goethe: "oh moment stay, thou art so fair." But more commonly what is felt to be a good thing isn't

now an actual fact, but a mere possibility in the future—as
when we climb a mountain to have the joy of a vast panorama, or when we work to solve a problem for the love of
knowledge as a good in itself. In these instances the trend of
the good to emerge from possibility to fact is the more striking. Let us then take a simple commonplace example of such,
and see how the urge-to-be reveals itself. And note that we are
not asserting that the self-realizing power always succeeds.
Goods conflict, some have less attraction than others. Commonly the more attractive prevails over the less, as the example we shall give makes clear. Also our free choice *may*
decide to let the less attractive prevail. (We shall later justify
our assertion of free choice, we here simply assume it as does
common sense.) And some good things we want we can't
get, owing to nature's laws—as when we long for warmth on
a bitterly cold day, though even then we wear a thick coat to
be as warm as we can. Sometimes, too, we feel the goodness
of something we know we can't possibly get in any degree,
and we don't even try to realize it. You would love to have
that very costly new car, but your salary won't permit it. Even
so, if some friend left you in his will a thousand or more
dollars, you would try to buy it. There is a *latent* urge even in
the goodness of what we know is beyond possible realization
as things are.

To be sure, you may here object that what is *felt* to be good
isn't always *really* good, so what we are here arguing doesn't
apply to what the above title declares. We shall meet this
objection later. But come now to the commonplace example
we spoke of.

You are hungry. You are at the breakfast table. Before you
are two dishes: a poached egg on toast, a slice of fried blue-
fish. Which will you take? The egg, you feel sure, will taste
good; the fish you don't happen to like, which means that it
will not taste good. So you choose the egg on toast. What led

you to choose it? The goodness of the taste. That good taste isn't a fact before you eat the egg; it is only a possibility, a possible shall we say. What turns this possible into a fact is the goodness of it. That goodness lures you into the choice, thereby makes itself real.

An Objection

Oh no, says the objector, your point of view is quite wrong. You are treating the possible good as if it were a kind of entity exerting power of itself. It is no such thing. It is you the hungry eater who generates the good. If you had already had a full breakfast and the egg on toast were offered you, it would have the same taste if you ate it, but the taste wouldn't be a good thing—because you wouldn't want it. *Your wanting* that taste is what makes it good. Always it is *your desire* that makes the good good. Hunger is what the psychologists call a drive; without that drive no food would be good. As many of our psychologists and philosophers declare, so it is with anything we feel to be good. Whatever is for us human beings a good thing is good because of some drive in *our* make-up, it is *we* that determine the good and realize it. Drink is good because we are *thirsty,* exercise is good because we *crave* using our muscles, rest is good because we *love* its refreshing feeling, money is good because it enables us to buy things we *want,* friendship is good because we have a native *drive* to companionship, sex-love is good because we have an inborn *drive* to sexual union—and so on. The good doesn't in the least tend to realize itself; *we* tend to realize it, that tending is what *makes* it good. Our inborn constitution *creates* our values. Our drives are born in us, inherited from our parents, with perhaps a mutation or two of our own. Only real things have power and urge; ideals wouldn't influence you at all unless you felt them, had a drive toward them. See how the goods differ with different kinds of animals! The drives that animate a cobra aren't much like those that provoke a man to study and reason. The very fact that these goods so often conflict, yes, even within and between human beings, shows that the good is wholly dependent on the make-up of the animal for whom it is good. Good is by itself, of itself, nothing; it is wholly relative to the animal drive. It is, as we say, subjective, nothing at all out there.

Yes, the claim we have been making would seem to take the good as a sort of Platonic idea, something self-subsistent, objective, a power working to realize itself in the world of phenomena. Surely for our modern empirical-science attitude this is nonsense. And even if we were right in asserting the power of the good once it is *felt* to be good, where is the evidence that possible good things tend to make themselves felt? If their urge-to-be comes only when they happen to be felt, doesn't that show them to be wholly due to the given biology and psychology of the animal which feels them? Surely it is up to us to show a trend of undiscovered possible good things to make themselves felt as time goes on. How could we possibly do this?

Evidence From Evolution

Well, there is the *fact* of biological evolution, and of progress therein toward more and more good things. More and more good things have become sensed, felt, desired, and many of them have thereby become realized. The goods for the lower animals can't compare in their quantity and intensity with those of the higher vertebrates, especially those of mankind. Even early man didn't begin to have anything like the number and depth of the goods we have today. Particularly is this true of what we call the moral goods. The idea of world-wide peace came on the scene only very late in the long course of human history. And think of the incredible number of our kindly charities today, as we noted above, in the wealthy U.S.A.—nothing like it ever before.

True indeed, you may answer, but also there are more evils today than ever before—more worries, uneasiness about the future, mental sickness, juvenile crime, and, above all, the terrible power of the destructive bombs. Why, then, if you are going to resort to historical evidence to defend your argument, mustn't you admit that the bad, evil, shows as much trend to be realized as the good? We might reply, perhaps it does; all we are concerned to show is that the good does so. But that reply isn't enough for our thesis. It might still be the case that the evils will in the end be stronger and overcome the goods—wherefore the good would *not* in the long run be self-realizing. But our thesis implies that while the good tends to realize itself, evil being the frustration of good thereby tends to abolish itself. The proper answer to the above objection is that what was felt as good to past mankind and therefore *was so far* good, often turned out to have more evil, too, in it than was felt at the time, and mankind slowly, gradually, came to realize more goods which did not have as much evil within them. After all, good things may contain evil as well as good —evil so far as they conflict with other goods and tend thereby to frustrate them. Such were many of mankind's earlier goods—for instance, one nation conquering others to increase its own wealth and power. Only of late has mankind come to see that such felt goods lead to frustration of many other felt goods and therefore are on the whole bad. And so it is with our increasing evils today—if they really are increasing—we are trying more and more to overcome them, however without succeeding as yet.

After all, why for instance do these youths commit their juvenile crimes? Because those crimes feel good to them, give them pleasure. They *enjoy* beating the people they dislike, envy, hate. They *enjoy* getting the things they steal, and so on.

To say that evils are realizing themselves more than ever today
is only to say that there are more *conflicts* between felt goods.
And on the other hand, we are certainly more aware of these
conflicts today than ever before and we are thereby trying
harder to find ways of abolishing them—abolishing the fights
between individuals, between groups, nations, races. This ap-
parent increase of evils makes us realize more acutely that
such evils must be destroyed, thus is the tendency of the good
to be realized grown stronger. Yes, it is dawning upon mankind that universal peace and love are very great goods, and
on the whole, however many the exceptions, we do sense and
feel more than ever in the past that these goods must somehow
be realized. They have an *appeal* to us, strong and increasing.
The conflicts between felt goods must cease! Our feelings must
be educated to sense goods which will not conflict with one another. There enters the key-good, as it were, each good not
hindering but rather helping to realize all the others as well as
itself—the gospel of love is the best name for it, as we shall see.

So now we ask, how do you account for this great overall
trend—impressive just because it has emerged in spite of the
long, long ages of obstruction, almost as if it were gradually
overcoming all possible obstacles—how do you account for it
except by a power within the ideal good working toward its
own realization? A power is that which brings something into
being, and haven't all these goods been brought into being by
their *attractiveness* to the conscious minds which felt them?
There is the great significance of the *fact* of biological evolution, its very discovery but a late product of what it discovered,
and one of mankind's most cheering discoveries. Evolution is
the very slow trend of life toward a maximum good! However far from that goal is its highest product, man today, many
of us are sensing something of that maximum good. The
great religions with their teaching of the Golden Rule first
sensed it. To be sure, their disciples, assenting orally thereto,

didn't practice it by and large very much, but they are now coming to feel its power, its lure, as in what is called the "social gospel"—particularly in the West and of late increasingly in the East. The biologists, natural scientists as they are, have been concerned most with the physical processes of evolution, in the geological periods and their events. They haven't stressed the evolution of the good, rather the evolving of more and more complex life-forms. Darwin spoke of the *Descent of Man,* Henry Drummond later wrote *The Ascent of Man.* And we are now emphasizing as he did the *value* point of view. Doesn't that throw a light on the biologist's facts which hasn't been brought out as it should be? Isn't evolution itself the best evidence for our thesis that the good not only tends to realize itself when felt but tends to make itself felt? Think of the many many kinds of life, plant and animal, which have survived and prospered. Doesn't it begin to look as if evolution is the trend to bring forth all possible kinds, levels, degrees of life, each with its particular goods?

Another Objection

Oh no, says the objector, all this evolution was just a matter of chance, of chance-mutations happening that way, developing more and richer *drives* in living things. Of course, when human beings and animals help one another rather than fight one another, they are more likely to survive. Mutations occurred, the biologists tell us, in many directions, some favorable, some and probably many more working against survival. The love-mutation, if we may so call it, was favorable. Gradually as mankind *happened* to grow more intelligent, they came, some of them, to see this, and they preached the gospel of the Golden Rule. Those who first saw its value were the moral, the religious leaders: Confucius, Buddha, Moses, Jesus, Mohammed. But intelligence and religion were just lucky mutations. And think what a long time it took before they happened to

emerge. Even in human history some hundred thousand years
passed before any human beings came to see the survival-
value of the love-motive. In mankind's early ages power,
strength to defeat his rivals, seemed to be the good thing. The
strongest survived. But when at long last men came to see that
cooperation was better on the whole for survival—survival the
basic *drive*—they turned toward that, slowly and painfully,
little step by little step. See then: what made them feel its
goodness?

See then: simply the fact that it contributed to this basic
drive for continued life, full and happy. But this urge which
you call the love-motive, mutation as it was, might not, need
not, have occurred at all. Surely it didn't *have* to occur. If it
had a power of its own, why did it take ages and ages to show
itself? It doesn't follow from any law of physical nature that
we know of. It doesn't even follow from the nature of living
beings, of what it means to be living. Plants, even the highest
plants, have none of it; among animals it appeared, even after
the long ages of evolution, only in a very small number, the
higher vertebrates. Think how many more animals there are
of the bacteria, protozoa, porifera, echinoderms, coelenterates,
mollusks, arthropods, all taken together, than there are of the
birds and mammals. Only these last have it at all, and even in
mankind it hasn't been too widely appreciated.

And why did this odd mutation increase its strength in mankind? Why didn't it confine itself to just a few humans and
then die out because the combat-motive, love of power, killed
off those few? Of course because man by another mutation
had become *intelligent* enough to see that cooperation favored
survival. But why had there been this mutation toward intelligence? True, intelligence favors survival; but why have survival? Why didn't all life perish from the earth? We know of
no necessity, no law of nature verified by physical science,
which can explain why mutations toward increasing survival

must occur. We don't even know how or why life came on the scene, still less why the quality of value, of good, which is found only in conscious life, should suddenly appear. All we can say is, it just happened so. There are no inherent values, no goods, in the non-living world just by itself. Their very late appearance within that world as in conscious minds is surely unaccountable, just a matter of chance. We the scientific thinkers find no principle which could *make* goodness come on the scene and tend to realize itself.

In sum, says the objector, it is only because the *drives* which appeared when life came to be, *happened* to take this or that form, that particular goods emerged. There was no "principle of good" as you might call it, which brought forth life with its drive toward preserving itself and the later drives which *happened* to favor the same. There is no such thing as good in itself. Only the coming up of chance mutations, culminating in the entrance of conscious desire in living things, brought forth the category *good*. Good is anything but a power in the real world, even in the world of living beings.

The Answer

But now come back to the example we gave at the beginning, an instance of conscious desire dictating the food we choose. Let us then examine this fact, conscious desire, wanting something we haven't yet got. What is that something? As we said, it is a possibility, a possible. What then is it, to desire a possible? It is to tend to make it real; but it is also more. Merely to tend to realize some possible, some potentiality in the present situation, is not by itself enough to bring in the factor of good. A ball rolls down the hill, it tends to reach the bottom, but there is so far nothing of good in reaching the bottom. If desire is *only* a trend or drive of the living organism toward a certain state there is no felt good about it. *Felt,* notice. *Consciousness* is the crucial thing. A conscious desire has a vision, dim or clear, of the thing desired, a thing not real, only possible. It feels the goodness of that thing. That goodness is not an event which gives rise to another event; it isn't a case of the sort of cause and effect occurring when the billiard ball hit by the cue goes rolling on. The thing you desire isn't a real event, yet there is a causal connection between it as a mere possibility and your present movement, however slight that movement, to realize it. That causal connection comes from its goodness. Goodness makes all the difference, goodness which comes only with consciousness. Its goodness is the fact that it *would* suit you, *would* gratify your want. But the suiting and the gratifying are due, not to the existence of the thing desired, since it doesn't exist, but to its naure, its character. It is that character which makes you want it, the goodness in it which gives it a power, a power which it possesses even as only a possible. *Possibles can and do have power in the realm of conscious life,* where values have emerged. Thus appears the difference between a drive and what we call a lure. A drive is a push from behind, a lure is a pull, a draw from ahead. Consciousness can include the presence of what is not yet, what is possible, what can be drawn by the possible future. Perhaps that is why, the future being not yet real, when we are drawn by the lures of conflicting goods we can choose between them. We can't choose about what is realized, as in the past; only as to the possible future. Of course we are so constituted that only certain possible events and no others will be felt as good—there lies so far the truth of the drive-concept. But a *mere* drive is just an efficient cause and contains no notion of the future possible exerting an influence. It is the fact of consciousness, which surveys alike past, present, and possible future, which brings to light the power of some mere possibles, the power we call goodness, to promote their realization in us.

So comes the conscious mind to feel, to see when it reflects, that the good ought to be—whence arise, as mankind evolves, the moral codes. Hence the truth of the saying: "the good is its own excuse for being."

We spoke of evolution as the *fact* that the sum total of goods has increased through the ages. Is there then anything in the above analysis to show that this increase is more than a matter of happy-go-lucky mutations? That there is something in the very nature of goodness which leads possible goods as yet undiscovered to be revealed, to make themselves felt and thereby realized?

Good, Once Born, Grows

We answer yes, there is that something. To see it, begin by noting this: there is an urge in the nature of the good, once it is felt and realized in our human life, toward self-increasing. The presence of some good lures us to seek more and more good not yet discovered. We want progress, advance—that means more goods, less evils. We want to know more and more about the universe, since knowledge is a good in itself. We want more health, less sickness, we want new and beautiful works of art, we want to preserve the fine old classics that they may be enjoyed more often by more people as time goes on. We enjoy our present goods, we want more of such. Human nature, whatever the stern moralist may say, wants pleasure, joy, happiness unlimited. So man has cooked up, as the Freudians declare, the idea of heaven, the all-pain-reliever, the soothing drug of perfect bliss, opiate of the people. The different ways to this as taught by the prophets are the different religions.

Yes, there is that in the experience of the good, no matter how limited, which lures to the gaining of more good and more good as yet undiscovered, abolishing all that frustrates, frustration being the mark of evil. Indeed, all conscious beings do want all the good they can get, though only the higher animals, perhaps only self-conscious man, have some inkling of the fact. The good, once felt, has thus a trend to self-increase, since it is so pleasing that it leads to the search for as yet unknown goods. Thereby these undiscovered goods, mere possibles not yet even felt, show their lure. As the Thomists say, the good is self-diffusing, *sui diffusivum*. And when the reflecting human being finally comes to see that the good is what ought to be, he sees that this means: promote the welfare of all conscious beings to the utmost possible—the moral principle of universal love.

Another Objection

But now again the objector. Even if you grant all this, it holds only *after* the consciousness of good has come in. What evidence have you that from the very beginning of life in its lowest forms there was implicit a trend, an urge, a force working to bring on conscious minds, minds which alone would sense the good and the bad? Of course, evolution *did* give rise to them, but why was this anything more than a lot of chance-mutations?

See then, we answer, how it was implicit in the nature of life, as contrasted with the non-living, to do so—and precisely *because* of the chance-mutations native to life.

How Good Came On The Scene

What is the general principle which distinguishes the living from the non-living? It is this: to prolong itself, to survive in spite of forces which would destroy it, by reacting to those forces in ways of its own, ways not present in the inorganic world. When a giant meteor falls to earth and smashes a rock to bits, the rock does nothing new, so to speak, to preserve itself. The cohesion which holds the parts of the rock together is overcome by a greater force, and that is the end of the matter. In life, on the other hand, there is some reaction, however slight, however unsuccessful here and there, toward preserving itself. The little primitive amoeba, losing its energy more and more by its movements, reacts against the destructive trend by absorbing food, by nutrition. And when finally it is about to give out, its life is continued by reproduction, by its offspring which is a part of itself surviving. From the beginning life is more or less of a conflict between things that tend to continue and things that would destroy them, in which life originates some way of its own which overcomes the latter, at least sometimes. Living things, as we say, *struggle* for existence. Dead things don't struggle, don't evoke a *new* response to continue their being. All this is of course unconscious in the early stages, even in the highest plants which came much later. And the ways of reacting toward continued living increased through the chance-mutations in the offspring.

Well, this trend to self-continuing in spite of destructive forces has an *implicit,* a *potential* reference to the future, even in the unconscious. As some biologists have said, life looks forward, not backward. Life from lowest to highest forms, declares E. W. Sinnott, is goal-seeking (*The Biology of the Spirit,* Viking Press, New York, 1958). In the inorganic with its laws the past determines the present, the present the future. In life the future with its not yet realized lead toward continued life, determines *some* response, due to a chance-mutation, if you like. Only to a slight degree perhaps, and often without success. Of course there are hostile forces which the organism can't yet overcome—lightning, cold, disease and such. But however slight and ineffective, there is inherent, potential in the living thing, this note of continuation in the future determining to some degree the present reaction. The possible future lurks behind the scene, exerting its influence. And what is consciousness but the actual presence in the mind of the possible future—a physical impossibility which reveals the dualism of mind and body? Yes, conscious mind is potential, latent, in the very nature of life. But what makes it explicit, actually in living beings? It surely isn't a necessity. Plants, highly evolved as they are, reacting as they certainly do to destructive forces, don't have it. Why should animals have it? Why indeed should life evolve at all? Why did new ways of reacting to hostile forces crop up, leading finally to conscious animals? We can't give any proof, can we, that there was such an entity as goodness lurking behind the scenes, waving its wand over the succession of living beings to make some of them, the animals, conscious of what they want.

Look again at the process of evolution. It is the *fact* that life through the long ages did find more and more ways of preserving itself. True, also, that life found more ways of destroying itself, as the animals came to prey on one another and man fought man as well as the beasts. Even so, the amount of life did increase up to its incredible extent today. True again, many of the mutations were unfavorable, leading to extinction, as the biologists tell us. There would seem to be no principle dictating that the mutations *must* favor life's continuing. Rather it looks as if there was through the ages a tendency to produce all possible mutations, good, bad, indifferent to life's aim, only the fit surviving. As the eminent biologist George Gaylord Simpson says: "Evolution seems to have tried out almost every conceivable possibility" (*The Meaning of Evolution,* Yale University Press, New Haven, Conn., paperback reprint, 1960, p. 40, footnote). Life was, as it were, an experiment trying this that and the other mutation, practically about all possible mutations, to preserve itself. As another biologist has put it: "Life seems to have explored every possibility and has made use somewhere or other of nearly every material available on the surface of the earth" (J. A. V. Butler, *Inside the Living Cell,* Basic Books, New York, 1959, p. 35). Later we shall make much of this; it is, we shall see, a principle at the very heart of reality, to realize all possibles permitted by nature's laws. And isn't that the same thing as chance? Isn't that why it is right to say that the mutations which brought about the advance in evolution are chance-mutations? For what does chance, as now understood, mean? It means—as we said—the gradual realization of all possibles, as when you toss a number of coins and as you go on tossing them all possible combinations of head and tail are realized, and realized with no preference. Each combination of head and tail is realized as many times as its relative numbers of head and tail permit. Yes, the objector is quite right when he declares the entrance of value, of good and bad in the course of evolution, to be just a matter of chance. But notice that chance today has a positive meaning for the scientist. We said it in Chapter I. No longer does it mean that *anything* may happen, no telling what. Rather it means that *everything* will sooner or later happen in a given realm of events which is not ruled out by the nature of that realm. So in the realm of living things, with their basic trend to continue even against destructive forces, about every possible way has been tried, every possible mutation so far and doubtless more to come. Certainly this principle of *positive* chance does seem to be at work in life's evolution. Look again at the universal life-trait, reproduction. Earliest forms of life, little, simple and weak, would surely have disappeared if they hadn't produced offspring. Reproduction would seem inevitable if life was to continue. And with offspring came the possibility of variation, of mutation, a possibility which was realized. Moreover it was realized increasingly when reproduction became sexual. The offspring, originally a part of the one parent which divided itself, was now a part of each parent, whereby it could vary more from each than if it were the product of one parent alone. So the area for mutations increased itself.

Yes, it looks to have been implicit in life's trend to continue

itself that mutations would enter the scene and would themselves increase and multiply. But why this particular mutation,
conscious mind, which is so utterly unlike any physical
change? How could it be introduced into a purely physical
realm except by some Divine intervention, some miracle? We
said it was a potentiality in life because of life's tendency toward preservation in the possible future. But what brought it
out into the light? Or put it this way: why did life divide itself into plants and animals, consciousness being found only in
animals?

How Consciousness Could Come In

See then: there are two possible ways in which living things
might preserve themselves against destructive forces. Motion
and rest are two basic attributes of physical being. Why not
then have some living things which preserve themselves by a
power of restoring and increasing their own substance *without*
moving, or with a minimum of motion? And why not another
group which save their lives by moving to avoid oncoming
danger, to capture food not directly at hand? Surely if life
tends toward maximum possible mutation it would come to
divide itself thus. And as we shall see anon, this division is
highly favorable not only to the continuation of life, but also
to the increasing goods of life—a most striking instance of the
good more and more realized.

At any rate, the division occurred. Green plants maintain
themselves by making their own substance out of what is
immediately at hand—sunlight energy, air, water, chemicals
in the soil, all touching the plant body. They don't have to
move to get their food from a distance; animals do move to
get it, to a greater or lesser extent. Typically, animal life is
moving life, moving toward or from this rather than that, be it
toward food, flight from a coming foe, and such—involving
the influence of the distant, the *away,* something away from,

absent from the living body. Mustn't the animal feel the presence of the object away from it? Be *aware* of it? *Awareness* goes with *awayness.* Isn't consciousness just the hereness to some degree of the there? Indeed, we shall see later (in Chapter IV) that there is something in the very nature of matter itself which make possible the mutation to consciousness.

True, many animal responses are but a physical stimulus provoking a fitting movement without any consciousness of the distant, as when some reflex action takes place. But not all. And as life became more complex with its increasing mutations, higher forms of animal life could hardly have failed to enlarge the sphere of awareness, and conscious mind became more and more helpful to survival. And note this: it was the primal trend, native to life, to continue its own being, which when accompanied by the need of movement to goals not immediately present, gave to the mutation to conscious mind a realm of *values,* things *wanted,* goods. The latent potential good in the unconscious aim of all life made itself explicit when animals with their pursuit of the distant became conscious of what they wanted and moved to get. Thus did the possible good make itself felt and realized in the field of conscious mind.

The Entrance Of Goods From Outside Animal Life

But life's inherent trend to realize possible goods hasn't confined itself to animal goods quite apart from the plant kingdom. There is indeed no good in the unconscious *just by itself.* A stone isn't good, a tree isn't good except as it *contributes* to what the conscious mind feels to be good. Yet this self-realizing of the good, implicit in the nature of animal life, doesn't exclude plant life from playing its part therein. In fact we could go much further, and later we shall do so, and see that the non-living world, valueless as it is in its merely material being, has also its great contribution to the good. But we are

now considering only the arena of living things. Look then at
the way in which the plants have contributed to the realizing
of what is good. Goodness applies to both kingdoms of life, to
each in its own way. Indeed, if it were limited quite to conscious animals, how could it be a *basic* potentiality of life?
Remember that there are many, many more plants than animals in the world. Is there then a sense in which the good is
self-realizing in the plant?

There is, and it shows itself in two ways. First, the plants
contribute to the animal goods as food. All animal food in
the end comes from plants. They are so far the source of good,
and what is the source of good is to that extent good. Not all
plants of course, some are poisonous, many have no lure for
the hungry animal. As we saw, it is characteristic of life to
vary in countless ways; many mutations are from life's point
of view failures. But when the animal has by happy chance
discovered that this or that plant does give him the food he
wants, he seeks it, he would have more of it, and in man he
cultivates it. Agriculture arrives, thereby increasing the plant
contribution of good. More and more does man use it to continue his life.

And secondly, plants give to the animal good not only to
continue its living, but also to enrich that living. That gift is
beauty. Beauty, to be sure, exists so far as we know—at least
as object of aesthetic contemplation—for mankind only,
though the higher animals do take pleasure in taste and smell,
if you want to call that an experience of beauty. For that matter, so does man when he senses exquisite tastes as a "gour-
met", and the like with odors. But we are here speaking
especially of beauty as the contemplative good, typical of mankind's vision of the plant world. Yes, it is one of man's best
gifts, and plant-life provides it. True, there are other beauties
—there are graceful animals, there is the beautiful sunset, and
so on. Also for man there is the beauty of woman, strongest of

lures to possess and protect. Yet on the whole animals stand more for power in movement, for *getting* what they want, plants more for still quiet beauty, *offering* what they have to help not only the continuing of mere life, but also for conscious minds as in mankind to develop the higher, more spiritual realm of the aesthetic, the contemplative phase of mind. And like other goods, this good of the plants is self-increasing. It stimulates us to cultivate it in gardens, we grow more and more lovely flowers and trees as good to look at. So the plants come to increase their own way of goodness by their attraction to the highest product of evolution, mankind. Such is the successful mutation distinguishing plants from animals, each helping the other to more and better life.

Well, we have been dwelling on the increase of good, and the evidence seems strong. But how about the increase of evils, which we mentioned above?

Have Evils Also Increased?

So now comes the objection from the fact of evils due to mutations. As we saw, probably most of the mutations were not successful; they killed off the animal and the plant. Doesn't that mean the increase, the self-realization of the bad? Certainly from the point of view of life's inherent trend to continue it is bad, failure, self-destruction. It is as if life were more inclined to destroy itself than to continue itself. Or we might state the matter thus: life differs from non-life in having its own original ways of reacting to forces acting on the living body, not at all with a trend to survival or to destruction, but quite indifferent to the result, just chance-mutations of all sorts, no matter what the result. Naturally the result would sometimes be survival, sometimes destruction. But surely there is no slightest suggestion in the fact of chance, that possible goods have a power *in themselves* to be realized. And even if that were the case, it would be just as true to assert that possible evils have a power in themselves to be realized. Above all, isn't the destruction of a *conscious* living being just straight evil? All conscious animals die; the more are born, the more die. And in the earlier stages of our human civilization, as also, alas! in our overpopulated undeveloped nations today, the more are born the more die without even growing to maturity. Life's inborn tendency to increase and multiply is all the more frustrated. Yes, even in the most civilized nations today we are repeatedly warned that population is increasing beyond the capacity of our earth to provide its needs for food and other things. Even in the higher plants, notice the tremendous waste going on—how few of the seeds in our common trees today have even a chance to survive and grow into new trees. As a particularly impressive example, witness the vast number of seeds produced by one of our largest trees, the sycamore, and see how few indeed of those which fall to the ground survive. Such waste is but a vast frustration of life's upward trend, from life's point of view a very great evil. You may say no, it is a good thing, because there wouldn't be room for them if they all grew up into trees. But the bad thing is that so many of them were produced, only to be frustrated.

Nor is this wastefulness confined to plant-life only. It is even more the case in animal life, especially in the higher forms. How many of the male sperms which enter the female womb succeed in fertilizing even one ovum? Typically, normally, only one of the many thousand sperms does so. All the others are lost, wasted, destroyed. Yes, if we assert, as we did above, that the essence of life as distinct from non-life is the trend to preserve itself, then the power of evil to realize itself is far, far greater than the power of good to do so. To put it even more strongly: if life's basic trend is to continue, then evil *always* triumphs over good, since all living things die, and in the higher forms more die before reaching a ripe old age and thus are prevented from having their possible goods realize themselves in a long life. The arena wherein possible goods actually realize themselves, as compared with the vast extent of life, is a very small one, even in the realm of conscious animals. How then can we say that it is intrinsic in life that the bad will decrease while the good will be preserved and increased, confined as this is to so small a region of life? No, there is nothing peculiar to goodness more than to badness or indifference, that leads to its realization. Haven't we been telling just a Pollyanna story?

The Answer

But now recall what we said at the beginning of this chapter. We repeat it: "we are not asserting that this self-realizing power always succeeds . . . some good things are prevented by nature's laws." As the two biologists quoted above tell us, it is as if life with its chance-mutations was an experiment, *trying* every possible mutation to preserve itself, to bring forth in itself what would when consciousness emerged be more and more goods. *Of course* it couldn't succeed every time with the forces of the inorganic being what they are. Life, weak and tiny at first, *must* be very slow in adapting itself to the environment while as yet it had no conscious knowledge of nature's laws; the chance-process was the only sure way, trying every possible experiment, to reach success. But it *was* a sure guarantee of success sooner or later. Always *some* mutation must succeed where all possible mutations occur. And that means that the good *must* be realized eventually, no matter how often it was prevented time and again.

Yes, provided no great external force comes in to kill all life, it is a logically necessary result of the given empirical fact, the chance-motive at work in life's inborn way of reproduction—itself one way of overcoming the great enemy, death—a necessary result that one success in preserving itself must sooner or later give rise to another and another and

another, increasing its extent more and more till the last
great step comes up, conscious mind with its goods being
realized more and more. No matter how many the failures as
time went on, the successes, no matter how few, would open
the way to more successes. If chance is the gradual realization
of *all* possibles then life with its chance-mutations—which the
biologists have told us are just about all the possible ones—
can't help but realize the ones which will preserve it, and in
more and more ways, thereby enlarging the content of the
living being, and sooner or later consciousness must enter the
scene, at length giving the mutation to intelligence which
finds new ways of life. And when with intelligence there also
emerges a greater *sensitiveness* to the many persisting evils
of life—a possible mutation which must sooner or later
occur—the urge to abolish the evils and increase the goods
becomes strong indeed. Thus the chance-mutations inherent
in life *mean* that possible goods not yet discovered are as it
were lurking behind the scene, awaiting their opportunity
to emerge into the light—all because chance means the realization of all possibles open to the nature of the situation.

And such is in fact the case with mankind today. By and
large we are much more sensitive to life's evils than ever
before, realizing as so many do today the badness of our
fighting instinct, of ignorance, poverty, disease, and such.
Even if the evils are increasing today, that only makes us
more eager to remove them. Our ideals of peace, cooperation,
health, abundant life for all, these are pressing on us more
and more. No matter if we can't realize them very much
now; we feel their *draw,* their urge, as never in the past.

And we must note in passing that much of what the last
objection called evil isn't really evil—the waste, the destruction of seeds, of germs. These are not evil, since they occur
in the unconscious. On the other hand they are very revealing of nature's way in life. They show much the same trait

as we have been emphasizing in respect of the chance-mutations. It is as if the reproductive phase of living organisms
produced as many seeds, germs, or eggs as possible. And
the fact that most of them perish is in line with the fact that
so many, if not most, of the mutations are failures. For that
matter, even if these wastes and failures were evil, they have
vanished—so far evil has destroyed itself!

Indeed, if we are as empirically minded as we should be,
we can hardly fail to see that the way we normally feel about
the good verifies the thesis here argued. When we come to be
aware of the goodness in some possible thing or event, we just
so far become aware of its lure, its magnetic draw urging us
to realize it. We *experience* directly its urge, we *feel* that it
should *be,* that it ought to be, even if it isn't in *our* power
to cooperate with its urge. Every possible good, by the very
goodness it contains, has a draw to be realized, a draw which
we discover within it when it dawns upon our conscious
minds.

Yes, even if we see that it can't be realized in this given
world, we have a feeling that somehow there ought to be a
world in which it can be realized—perhaps in the future of
this world, perhaps in some other kind of world. There is the
origin of our notion of *perfection*—hence the native trend of
us human beings to religion. We *feel* that somehow, somewhere, there ought to be, there *must* be, a realization of the
perfect good, that it is intrinsic in the nature of the good to
be. And as it can't *be* in *our* imperfect world, mustn't it *be* in
some other realm? *That* is the source of mankind's religion;
not, as the skeptics declare, our subjective drive, cooking up
the "opiate of the people". Religion, worship of the Perfect
Being, God, dawns on mankind because of their dim sense,
not yet brought into the clear light, of the inherent trend
of the good to be. No, we don't cook up religion, it dawns

on us like the rising sun whose rising we can but accept. In the chapters to follow we shall see the significance of this.

So far we have been looking at the general course of evolution, bodily and mental, as witnessing the increase of good things in this life of ours. We used the term good, in a somewhat vague rough sense, as that which lures to the realizing of whatever is felt or comes to be felt as desirable. It was applied indiscriminately to such different things as food, health, rest, exercise, beauty, knowledge. But now comes forth another objection, quite different from the naturalist empirical ones above.

The Objection Of The Strict Moralist

This objector dwells in a lofty region above and even opposed: he says we haven't been treating of what is *really* good. The real good, he insists, is what the moral law dictates. These worldly fleshly goods aren't the real thing. The *felt* good is *not* necessarily good. We said above that we would meet this objection, namely that we are confusing the felt good with the truly good—and it is the stern moralist who confronts us with it. Only the righteous moral code, he affirms, tells us what is the truly good. And that good just does *not* tend to realize itself. It can be realized only by our resolute free choice, no lure about it. It is as it were a command from on high, from God if you please, at any rate from a spirit-level far above the pleasures of everyday life. It fights again and again with those pleasures, the flesh wars with the spirit. If you think it tends to realize itself, look at the increasing crimes today, the growing juvenile delinquency, above all the world wars larger, more destructive than any wars of the past. No, the moral good, the doing of what is right just because it is right, is showing us today that its realizing depends wholly on *us*, on our free and resolute choice alone. It is anything but a self-realizing power.

This objection is very helpful, as it leads us to consider what morality really is and to see that it is not the stern command alleged, but is that consummate good which we all really do want—the road to maximum enjoyment by every-one of all possible goods, none conflicting. In short, it is the love-motive. The moral law with its *Ought,* its *Should,* comes from the *Would,* what we *would* have if we could. Morality does at first look like a harsh dictation, and that stage is a necessary one to a degree, but as we humans progress we come to see that it is a loving urge, an urge to a universal love which is a joy in itself and in its results, a trend of the maximum good to be realized by us all. Now to see this.

Origin And Meaning Of The Ought

After all, we do use the same word *good* when we speak of the moral law as when we speak of a good dinner. We can't help it. There must be *some* kinship between the noble self-sacrifice of the soldier to save his country and the pleasure of a good meal. What is it then?

Moral behavior, most of us would agree, is doing something we freely choose to do. There is nothing compulsory about it. Typical is the case of temptation. You are tired out, you long to sit still and do nothing. Rest is felt as good. Yet you know that your sick friend a mile away would be greatly cheered and even improved in health if you went at once to see him. If you do go, you do what is right. But you wouldn't have the credit of doing right if you hadn't *chosen* to do it; and the harder the choice, the more credit to you. Shall we say: there wouldn't be any morality unless there were conflicting goods? Well, what does conflict mean? It is the meeting of two opposing forces. The temptation to sit and do nothing is an urge, a lure. It can be opposed only by another urge, another lure. No, you say, it is opposed only by your free choice. But what is such a choice? It is between the alternatives which you are considering. A choice is not itself an urge, a draw; it is a concentrating on one of two urges, letting that one have its way. Your will is no creative force in itself. There has long been a delusion here. You choose to go out to your sick friend, but you don't by your will *alone* make yourself walk. You couldn't walk unless your leg-muscles worked all right. The laws of physiology *gave* you the power to walk. It is of fundamental importance for us to understand that our wills do nothing by themselves alone except *choose between urges*. A difficult choice is one against a stronger urge, a stronger lure, an easy choice is for such a lure. Against the stronger it is hard to concentrate attention on the lure of the weaker. But all the will does is to fix attention on the chosen alternative and let it have its way.

The will is like the little switch which by moving just the least bit turns the mighty force of the speeding train in this or that of two possible directions. So we must say that the morally right deed is *felt* by the chooser to have its lure, its appeal, an appeal resisted by what we call the temptation. And if the moral good has its appeal, so far it does tend to realize itself, however weakly, however often the appeal is overcome because the sinner chooses to concentrate on the lure of the opposing possible deed and let it have its way. The stern moralist does feel that the good ought to be, and the oughtness of it is just its felt goodness; it is no less a felt lure than is the temptation which lures against it. The only distinction you can make between the right and the wrong must then be that the right is a greater, deeper, more lasting good than the good which conflicts with it.

These modern "emotivists" as they are called, are quite correct when they declare that the right is what we approve, and as we approve it we want it to be realized by you and me and so we say "do it"! Of course the trouble is that we differ in our approvals, our goods conflict. What the moral law urges is that the greater and more lasting good *should* be chosen rather than the lesser goods which oppose it. It is what we *would* choose if we understood clearly all that it means. And it isn't too easy to realize what it means, because, as the strict moralist would put it, the more immediate goods of the flesh have a stronger appeal. That is why, when the moral consciousness, so to call it, dawns in mankind, some additional motive must be found to help us choose the right. Man resorts to his religion, declares that God the Supreme Power will reward you if you do the right and punish you in hell if you don't. The early stages of morality have to stress this power-motive, morality as a command, a hard discipline, moved so largely by fear of punishment. And note that even here the moral good is a *felt* good—it gives relief, escape from the dread torments of hell. Isn't escape from pain a felt good? And the greater the possible pain, the greater the good of escape. After all, what good is there in the good if it is never felt?

Yes, the fear-stage of morality has its place as educating the weak, the undeveloped. Isn't it like what we do when we discipline the growing child? He hasn't yet come to see that what he is told to do is for his own best good, and for the good of others too. So often it is disagreeable to him that he needs the reward-punishment motive. Even in our advanced religions today, Christianity, Judaism, Islam, the fear-motive persists with many disciples. Do right or go to hell! But on the other hand mankind is now passing, or tending to pass, beyond this primitive stage—to realize that the love-motive is good in itself, that God the Supreme Power is the Supreme Lover and longs to bring us all to heaven, if we would but permit His love to enter our hearts.

Not, of course, that this love-motive demands that we go to the other extreme and abolish the discipline so needed today for our youth, and not that we can yet afford to discard the punishment-motive for the murderer, the cruel sadist and such. When we begin to sense the beauty of the love-urge we tend to be so entranced by it that our emotion excludes quite the discipline-motive and we think of punishment as vindictive, as vengeance, which of course it is not. Love at first is so often misdirected! And misdirected it is today when we fail to punish the youth-gangs who beat up and kill, the schoolboys who fight their teachers.

But we are now speaking of the basis of the moral law, the lure within it which gives its self-realizing trend more and more as we grow to feel the same. Love, as we said and shall later stress, is the urge to promote all possible goods to all conscious beings, without any conflicts between them. When the lure to the morally right is seen and felt to be this love-motive whose fulfillment is a joy in itself, there will be no need to dwell on the power-motive, the command to do or be punished. Then the right, good in itself, will be more and more self-realizing, will require little or no struggle, to be settled by a hard choice of the will. For the love-motive there is no fear, no will-struggle. Love comes to see that the ought, so emphasized as unique by moralists past and present, is really but the lure of the good, of all possible good to all, to realize itself. It is no longer a command, it is a joyous trend. And isn't this actually the case today with many of us, as we have come to do kindly deeds just from the longing to help those in misery—no struggle of the will at all? That is what the genuine morality will become.

Yes, doesn't it look as if every good of every sort open to man and beast, from the lightest good of scratching an itch to the high and lasting goods of the social arena, tends to realize itself? It may be quickly or it may be with long long delay. It seems to be the very nature of life, with its chance-mutations as if in every possible direction, that more and more goods would do so.

The Definition Of Good: Its Wide Extent

May we then, in sum, define the term *good* thus: it is that which by a trend of its own alone tends to pass from the possible to the actual more and more, in the realm of conscious beings. To be sure, this seems to limit the extent of goods to a very minute quantity—how few are the conscious minds as compared with the multitude of merely physical beings, the non-living things, the lands, the seas, the air, in fact the enormous, the incredibly vast material universe. We did see above that there is a great contribution to the goods of conscious life even in the realm of the unconscious plants— plants far more numerous than conscious animals, and giving us goods which by their attraction lure us to realize them more and more as says the definition. But even the plants are a tiny realm in comparison with the volume of our earth, still more so with the solar system—and so on as we proceed outward to the nebulae, and beyond. Yet recall that we also said above that we would later show how the inorganic also contributes to the goods of conscious life and thereby has its own contribution to goodness, giving us experiences whose goodness lures us to increase them. Let us now see this.

The Goods Of The Non-Living

The non-living region of our world gives us light, air, water, and other goods, helpful increasingly to life as it advances. But further: the terrific extent of the physical universe bestows on us humans certain higher goods, and these also increasingly. The law and order of the vast universe stimulates us more and more to know, to understand its laws, thus contributing to the advance of what many have deemed our highest faculty, intelligence. If plants give us the more immediate joys of food and beauty, the majesty of this outer realm gives an even stronger urge to progress than those more

immediate joys would arouse—witness the science of astronomy. Also the stimulus to increasing knowledge has, within
the area of our little earth, led to better understanding of the
nature of mere material being—discovery of the electrons,
protons, neutrons, etc. And in addition to all this, our scientific knowledge has given us many new immediate joys, the
benefits conferred by our machines. Knowledge is power, said
Francis Bacon, and power is good—to repeat from Chapter I.
True, these machines have their evils too; witness the increasing accidents by car and plane. Yet we all do agree that the
progress of science in the realm of the non-living is a very
great good.

There is here another good too. We love to contemplate
the great, the grand, the magnificent. *Grand* is a value-word.
How we love to view the majesty of the starry heavens! We
adore greatness—and the most obvious instance is the vast
space of the sky. The philosopher Kant, idealist though he
was, revered the starry heavens as he revered the moral law.
Nor is it the *mere* magnitude of the universe that we love to
contemplate. It is the greatness of its *order*. Order, object of
intellect's deep interest, is beautiful; and the vaster the order,
the more wonderfully beautiful it is. Is there not then something very, very good in the law-abiding mighty universe
around us? And notice what this law and order means. It
means that each physical process—the attraction of the sun,
the movements of its planets—*contributes* to the others what
they do, to a degree. As far as there is here an organic unity,
so far is there an *analogy,* even in the non-living, to the love-
motive. Why is order beautiful, appealing to the intellect?
Because the elements, as it were, *help one another* to show
what they can do. *Mutual* aid is there, even in its limited way.
And we conscious beings love to behold this analogy to the
beauty of mutual aid. Yes, we may rightly say that even in
the non-living there is that which, when we conscious minds

come on the scene, has realized a great goodness to us, a splendid contribution to our values. As thus a unique source of good, it has so far a good of its own. Isn't this a good realizing itself through the agency of the vast indifferent inorganic? No wonder that the writer of Genesis said of God viewing His creation: "And God saw that it was very good." And by the way, here is another answer to the objection we met toward the end of Chapter I.

And there is one more good, due to the presence of laws, in the non-living world about us. Laws enable us to count on what is coming, what will happen in the future, to plan successfully what we shall do. If there were no laws at all in nature, if anything whatever might happen, living beings with their ways of reacting to nature's forces couldn't preserve themselves. If the sun should decide not to rise tomorrow, if there were no law of gravitation to hold us down to the earth, if water should suddenly turn into sand, what would become of us human beings, of even the lower forms of life? The devout religious one might say: God established laws in the inorganic so that life as it evolved might learn to adapt itself more and more to the world around it. To be sure, this good contributed by the laws of our environment isn't of so majestic, lofty, spiritual a character as the goods we noted above. But, on the other hand, it is more fundamental to the very existence of living beings. Without those laws the living beings with their ingrained ways of behaving couldn't have continued, survived, very long, if at all.

But of course we shall be told once more that all this business of the good being realized may be as true as you please, but it still doesn't meet the objection that the whole process was just a matter of the chance-mutations which brought on at length conscious minds with their little area of good things. It wasn't the goodness due to the mutations that made them occur, it was just chance, no more. And there is no inherent good in chance, is there?

This brings us to what we shall later bring out as a fundamental point of the present book, indicated as it was by its subtitle. What is the significance of chance?

Chance Again Viewed

Let us repeat for emphasis what we said above. As the term has of late come to be understood, and as we here define it, chance is the realization of all possibles open to the given kind of event, no one instance determined by any other one, as is the case with causal laws. For instance, in tossing five one-cent coins, there occurs as it goes on an even distribution of the head-tail combinations according to the possible ways of combining. All heads can occur in but one combination, four heads and one tail in more, three heads and two tails in still more, and so on—and the ratios between these possible numbers of combinations are gradually realized equally as the experiment continues. The chanciness of each toss consists in the non-compulsion of the particular combination then and there. It is *not* compelled by any law *except* the law that with the given coins *some* one of the possible combinations must occur. This means that the particular combination is not caused by the one preceding it; rather, it seems to create itself, so far as the sequence of events is concerned. So far as any event is a matter of chance, so far it, as it were, creates itself, however shocking this may seem. Most of our scientists today, with their modern notion of statistical law, have accepted chance in the above sense, even if they don't speak of any self-creating. And we have admitted above that the mutations of evolution are chance-events. Doesn't this mean that they are self-originating? If so, as the mutations brought about at length, however slowly, the arena of the good, thereby the good was and is self-realizing. And the bad mutations destroyed life; destruction is not the realization of anything. So now we can seem to see *how* and *why* the good is self-realizing, passing of itself from the possible to the actual, self-creating if not opposed by a superior power. Within limits, of course; no event in our law-abiding world is *wholly* a matter of chance. And notice this: the good mutations enable life to continue, and so to originate more and more good mutations. The trend of the good is to realize more and more the possibilities open to living beings, to realize all possible traits of life. It is this self-creating character of the good which explains why when the conscious mind senses a possible good, that possible good is felt to have *in itself* a drawing power to become real. Hence if we examine the meaning of chance, is it not quite rational, not mysterious at all, that the good is self-realizing?

In fact, we now repeat, chance is a more positive trait of reality than law. What is a law? It is limited, restricted chance! Only such and such events, out of all conceivable possibilities, are permitted. Yet even nature's laws are not totally restricting, they are statistical, they permit chance-variations within certain limits. Yes, law is really more negative than positive. Chance, the trend to realize all possibles, is far more positive, more creative, than law. And the trend of evolution to realize all possible goods open to life is a far more positive affair than any particular law, as all such laws are restrictions. There isn't nearly as much in nature's laws as in the princple of chance with its creative novelties. And of these self-originating novelties the goods of conscious beings are the most striking. In them *value is the source of being,* their goodness leads to their being.

But now comes the great objection, dear to the hearts of all who have high respect for reason—a respect too which we have all along avowed.

The Rationalists Object

These objectors cannot admit that chance is anything like the fundamental principle we seem to make it. For everything that is, there must be a *reason why*. Indeed, even if most of our physicists today accept statistical laws rather than the rigid determinism of earlier science, they—some of them—feel certain qualms about the business. They have come to admit that physical science hasn't reached, perhaps never will reach, final absolute certainty. Always new discoveries will crop up, revealing the limits of past and present knowledge. See the book by Henry Margenau, *The New Faith of Science,* and especially the book by David Bohm, *Causality and Chance in Modern Physics,* which explicitly defends this claim against chances. It may well be, this scientist tells us, that no single law can be precisely fulfilled, just because it never works alone. Whatever it brings about is produced as accompanied to some degree at least by the action of many other laws, some already known to us, probably many more yet to be discovered in the endless progress of science. No, we can't be at all sure that the fact of statistical laws implies the presence of chance. That fact may well be due to the interaction of many many laws, each law rigidly determining its events if left alone, as in fact it never is or will be. After all, chance is irrational, isn't it? Reason *demands* a reason why; chance, taken as self-creation, is just a refusal to give a reason.

Well, before meeting this mighty objection, accusing us of cutting at the very roots of intelligence, let us note that the argument just given, referring to the interaction of many laws in each single event, does contain an implication of chance. If any one law is never exactly fulfilled, due to the action of other laws, aren't those other laws a matter of chance to the one law? Unless all the laws of nature can be reduced to one system, each law by its very nature implying all the others, it is still chance that they are all present together. And even if we could verify such a system, why that system and no other? But of course the objector would only say: it is your *duty* as an intelligent being *never* to stop with some particular system, order, given fact, or whatever. To accept chance is to commit intellect's unpardonable sin!

To meet this accusation, so obvious, so natural, so seemingly inevitable for the lover of intelligence, we must go more deeply into the meaning of chance than we have done so far. That we shall do in Chapter IV. So far, we might say, we are but preparing the way for the claims we shall there set forth. We have only been defending the thesis that the good, the value-realm, has a self-realizing trend which the doctrine of chance-mutations justifies. Later we shall see that the doctrine of rigid determinism does not, *cannot,* give the rational explanation of events which it claims to give.

Can Love The Supreme Good Be Self-Existent?

Now to see—as preparing the way further—the relation of our above arguments to the definition we gave of love. We said: love is the urge to realize all possible goods to all conscious beings. We saw how the structure and behavior of the physical universe does to a degree work that way—not only in the evolution of life on our little planet, but also in the incredibly vast realm of brute matter, however indifferent to good and bad it is apart from the beholder. Is not reality *so far* love's self-realization? Never mind how many other things there are, things as destructive to life as earthquakes, as indifferent as the expanding universe or the law of entropy; there is at least *something* of the power of love to reveal itself. Hindered though it is in our faulty realm on earth and beyond, it is there and more of it is there than is evident on the surface. But the main point is: we directly feel in our own experience this self-realizing power. As we experience it directly it is the inherent power of the good—really the love-urge—which by its goodness passes from the possible to the actual, from non-being to being. The good *so far* makes itself be, is its own excuse for being. That is why William James could say: "there is no problem of good."

No, it is not merely the causal laws of our material world, or the psychological laws of animal or human beings, which give the good its power to be. That power is revealed to us in our direct experience of getting what we like; it is the goodness of the good that does the work. And if those laws of the body and mind favor such, they, too, show the influence of the good. Often enough they don't, of course; that raises a problem we shall treat later, the problem of evil. Also, there too often comes up another factor—man freely chooses the lesser good which frustrates the greater. As we have said, the good by no means always *succeeds* in realizing itself. But all the same there *is* at work the principle of love, center and core of good, the *trend* to realize all possible goods to all conscious life.

Oh no, you say, love isn't a principle, an impersonal force. Love is just an emotion in a conscious being. The poet may declare that love makes the world go round, but poets delight in metaphors, they give no scientific truth. The fact is, you say, that there can't be such a force unless there is present a Great Person Who *feels* it. But we haven't proved that there is such a person!

Yet the objection overlooks the central point: goodness as we *feel* it, *experience* it, is a power in itself. It is no haphazard *result* of nature's laws, it is creative, it makes many things real which otherwise wouldn't be real! It moves itself, the possible good, into being. Its character, its essence, tends to its existence. Love, as we here define it, is thereby a principle, a power in itself, moving from essence to existence. If there were nothing to hinder it, its essence would *imply* its existence! But, let us add, that doesn't exclude it from being *also* an emotion in a conscious mind. And to see that it might be such, listen to a further suggestion.

We spoke of the maximum good for all. That doesn't imply the perfect realization thereof for us creatures. Mankind is imperfect, and doubtless always will be. But the trend of the love-urge toward the maximum, even in us, suggests something more, however wild it may look to our empirical-science attitude. May there not be a realm of being apart from this physical universe? May not the law of self-realization of the good imply that in such a realm, where there is nothing to interfere with the law, as there is in our physical universe, it must be perfectly fulfilled? As in a Perfect Being, a Being containing all possible goods, none conflicting, Supreme Love realized in its Supreme Intelligence, Supreme Power, Supreme Bliss? And our experience does reveal to us common limited human beings, something of such a realm apart. We experience joys that are not physical, in addition to those that are. We have bodily delights in eating, exercising, resting; we have also purely non-bodily joys, particularly in our human love-arena—spiritual we call them. The joys of knowledge and unselfish love are quite other than bodily affairs, we cannot but believe them spirit-facts. So the door is opened to the suggestion: is it not possible that in this region, however dimly sensed by us usually, there may be no interference, nothing to hinder the love-urge from realizing itself perfectly in a Being Who is therefore self-existent? Yes, this opens the door, it would seem, to a new form of the "ontological proof", so generally rejected even by the devout religious ones. It is the love-urge which does it—an approach through the principle of chance as the realizing of all possible *goods*—which has not been used, so far as we know. We shall claim that it shows us, not merely what we have already declared, that love *is* self-realizing, but *why* and *how* it *must* be self-realizing—all because chance as here defined is, we shall claim, an apriori logical necessity! And thereby we shall see that love is nothing beyond reason, but is a wholly rational affair. Love and reason are at bottom one.

We just said "this opens the door" to the ontological proof. But must we go through the door? Now to see that reason commands us to do just that.

CHAPTER III

WHY SEEK THE ONTOLOGICAL PROOF?

The Thomist Position

In the most thoroughly worked out system of Christian philosophy, Thomism, the being of God as First Cause of the existing universe is for reason a necessity. And as First Cause of the universe, He cannot Himself be caused; reason demands that He is self-existent. According to Holy Writ, God announced His self-existence when He said to Moses, "I am that I am." But finite human minds, so if we are correct the Thomist argument goes, cannot *understand* His self-existence. God alone, the Perfect Intelligence, can do so. We justify our belief in Him by reasoning from the *given fact* of the world's being. Apart from that given fact we have no *reasoned* proof of His existence; our reason can proceed only from what is, from *being*. We cannot understand how He as it were makes Himself exist. All our knowledge must start from given facts, from being. Indeed, didn't we with our demand for reason's rights argue above for the self-realizing of the good from the given facts of biological evolution? How could the trend of the love-principle to realize itself, to realize all possible goods, work at all unless there were already existing *beings* in which to realize those goods? And what those goods could be is determined by the *given* nature of those beings. No, we can't go behind the realm of given fact, especially in regard to the fact of God's being.

Indeed, why is there any being at all rather than nothing? The mystery of being, as it is called, is for us insoluble. Such if we are right, is the position of Thomism, most rational of theologies. And how many non-Thomist philosophers or theologians have even tried to solve that mystery? We know of but one, Paul Weiss—we shall later consider his proposed solution. Well, as we are to see in Chapter IV, to solve that problem is to solve the problem of God's self-existence, to see how and why God is self-existent, quite apart from His being the First Cause of this universe. Yes, the argument we shall give should, we claim, hold even for those thinkers who would deny the causal argument for God's existence.

Another Approach

Notice now, however, that there is a hint, a suggestion, even among the Roman Catholic philosophers, along with the Thomists, of another way of approach to the mystery of God's being. While the rationalist system of Thomism has long been declared the proper philosophy by the Catholic Church, there has also been among their philosophers and theologians another persisting trend, not denying the positive truths of that system, yet approaching the problems concerning God's being and nature along a different road. Recall, for instance, the teachings of Duns Scotus, Bonaventura, St. Francis, and Pascal. Their emphasis was not so much on reason as the proper road to truth; they stressed also the need of guidance by the emotional urge. We needn't now go into their systems; we but recall that in addition to the Thomistic rationalism there is still present this other "Franciscan" road to truth. Remember Pascal's words: "the heart has its reasons." Well, however he may have meant them to be above and beyond logical demonstration, we shall take these reasons to mean rational necessities revealed by the *emotional* life. We the *Agapologists* are respecting this Franciscan way. Coming to treat the mystery of God's self-existence as we are by understanding the meaning of *love,* by the value-road, we may see what the approach by reason along the straight and narrow path of given *fact* couldn't reveal. Perhaps the value point of view may reveal what the *being* point of view can't see. Didn't we see in the last chapter that the good—love, the very essence of the good—*has* realized itself, made itself *be,* where it didn't exist earlier? May there not be here a principle of self-existence at work in addition to, side by side with, the causal principle in the laws of nature? So let us see if we can't bring to light this principle, explain it, justify it.

For of course we haven't yet seen *why* the good is self-realizing and if nothing interferes must be *actually* realized. True, we did see that this self-realizing is the principle of chance at work, chance as properly understood today. But we didn't explain *why* there is this chance, this trend to realize all possible goods. We cannot *understand* the Divine self-existence unless we see why this principle of chance is a rational necessity *just by itself.* And if we can do this we *may* be able to answer the objection above noted, that there cannot be any good realized unless there are already on hand beings, or *a Being,* in whom to realize it.

Well, of course as we said, this concerns what the philosophers and theologians have called the ontological proof. And of all the reasoned arguments for God's being, that one has been the most frequently rejected. Why then?

Look at what might be called the classical form of it, one which at first glance seems quite reasonable: the argument of Anselm. He declared that God must be self-existent because He is by definition perfect, and perfection implies existence. Any ideal good which fails to *be* is so far lacking in power and therefore isn't perfect. To lack the power to *be* is to be weak and thereby imperfect. Yet the argument fails, according to Aquinas. True it is, he said in effect, that God wouldn't be perfect unless He existed, but what made Him exist? He is indeed perfect by His very definition, yes; but does the defini-

tion necessarily apply to a real being? Is He *really* perfect?
Or we might put it thus: if you *think* of God as perfect you
must *think* of Him as real, but that doesn't prove that your
thinking agrees with fact. True, you might reply that the existence implied by perfection *means* existence independent of
your thinking—but still you are only *thinking* of that existence as independent. The argument always needs a *witness* of
God's being. It is *not* by itself alone an ontological proof. It
has to appeal for support to the causal argument for God's
being, and the causal argument starts from the already given
existence of this world. The genuine ontological proof must
show that even if God hadn't created this world He still must
exist. It would seem to demand a proof, as it were, out of
empty air! Surely if your argument is to demonstrate a reality
it must start from reality. You can't get reality out of nothing!
Yes, the objection comes again: if love, the perfect good, is
self-realizing, there must be a being or beings in whom it can
realize itself. Being, existing things, must be ready at hand,
else there is nothing for love to work on. All our arguments
above for the power of love started from the *fact* that there
were and are living conscious beings in whom more and more
good did and does come to realize itself. Yes, the Divine self-
existence, independent of all that it has created, must remain
a mystery to us.

Reason's Demand

Yet we the defenders of reason in religion must not, cannot, rest content with a mystery even though our reason leads
us by the causal argument to believe in what the mystery declares. Knowledge, understanding, is a good in itself, and in
accord with what we said above about the moral law, all good
things so far as they don't frustrate other goods, ought *to be*.
Every mystery *ought* then to be cleared up, made intelligible.
It is our *duty* to seek to understand why God must exist apart

from anything He has created. Never rest content with what has been called a simple faith! Have that faith as a guide, yes, the faith that God is the acme of intelligibility, of logical necessity—it will help you to come nearer to seeing how He is so. But as faith without works is dead, never will it be right for you to stop your earnest quest for *knowing* God. Doesn't the All-lover want you to know more and more, above all to know Him better and better? The mystical experiment seeks to experience His presence, but it must not *exclude* the intellect which loves understanding as well as direct experience of fact.

Yes, Agapology with its doctrine of good—love the way of realizing maximum good—tells us that intelligence, itself a good, *ought* to progress more and more, not only as knowing the ways and laws of this given universe, but also as comprehending more and more of the Divine nature. And wouldn't it be the very deepest contribution to our reverence for reason, to see that it can be known why God *must* exist?

To be sure, we are here talking as if we already knew that He does exist. We are so far but addressing those who do so believe. We have as yet offered no proof, aiming as we are to show that independent of any causal or other argument for His being, God *must* exist. We are saying that if you do believe in God it is your duty to see why just of Himself, apart from anything outside Him pointing to Him, He *must* exist. Yes, for those who accept His being it is their *duty* to seek the ontological proof. But more: for those who doubt or deny it, yet do respect reason as do we who write this, it is their duty and our duty to solve the mystery of being—the solution of which, we shall see, gives the ontological proof itself.

An Objection

But now comes an objection from the devout believer, an objection against even the attempt. It is, he will say, too utterly presuming, what the Greeks would have called *hybris,* insolence. As the good orthodox Christian would say, no finite creature could possibly touch the deepest core of Divinity, His self-existence. The attempt is blasphemy! We can know His nature only by analogy at most—and there is in us *nothing* analogous to self-existence, created beings that we are.

Indeed we must admit much of this, but by no means all. It does not apply to love, to true genuine love. True, our human loves are weak, limited in degree and extent—that doesn't mean that they are a different *kind* of love from God's love. As the good Rufus Jones said, there is only one kind of love, however the *degree* of it falls short with us humans. Our degree of it is the extent to which God's love has entered our hearts; every genuine love is the presence of God in us to some degree. That is why there is no *hybris,* no blasphemy in saying we touch Him directly, sensing in Him the Perfect Lover, experiencing what otherwise we would fail to grasp. There is the Franciscan motive noted above—we would *add* it to the orthodox Thomist causal approach, not in the least denying that approach, yet valid even apart from it. Yes—to return to our claim—we do have in the experience of the possible good realizing itself, love the supreme good, an example of something making itself exist just by its own nature as a mere possible.

But now you ask: how can this be so? Everything that exists must have a cause, a reason why. All science is based on that. We can't *understand* how a mere possibility can *make itself real.* Science, knowledge, deals with given existence alone. But the point this overlooks is the value-approach of Agapology. What looks quite impossible for reason from the point of view of just *is* or *is not* doesn't look so from the point of view of the good, of value. There may be in the experience of value, of the good, of love, a way toward understanding how and why a mere possibility can make itself actual. We feel, we directly sense, something in what is a possible good, which turns it into the actual good. We don't feel that about any other trait of our experience. The devotee of reason has treated reason as *excluding* the testimony of emotion. But there is in our *feeling* a testimony which suggests a clue to what is for *exclusive* reason an insoluble mystery. It is a simple empirical evidence, quite satisfactory even to common sense —we aren't at all puzzled as to *why* we do what we like, what feels to us good. Yes—to repeat once more—it is the *goodness* of the possible just by itself that adds a *new* fact to what already exists. May it not then add a new fact to a realm where nothing already exists? Well, if we can see *why* we are not puzzled about our doing what we like, why the possible good thereby makes itself be, can we not then come to see why God the Supreme Good must exist?

Agapology, centered then on the realm of value, may find a way to solve the problem of God's self-existence which the mere study of fact, of being, couldn't reveal. For Agapology, ontology is axiology! Even Anselm's argument from *perfection* was drawn from the value-arena, though it assumed too much.

The late G. E. Moore, it will be remembered, declared that value, the good, couldn't be defined in terms of fact, of being *alone*. Agapology will agree to this, and will add that being *can* be accounted for in terms of value. Doesn't Thomism teach that *bonum*, the good, is a universal trait of being, a transcendental? And the highly esteemed axiologist, W. M. Urban, affirmed that existence is itself a value.

Agapology's Duty

Recall the saying: the good is its own excuse for being. As we said above, it was the warm-hearted William James who wrote "there is no problem of good." Indeed, something of the same in Western philosophy is as old as Plato with his *Idea of the Good.* He loved it, saw it as the ground of all that is. Yet he confessed, he couldn't explain it. Then Aristotle turned philosophy into the road of pure reason, largely neglecting the claims of the love-motive. His God wasn't much of a lover. He loved Himself, but didn't care much about His creatures. And as our human life evolved into devotion to intellect as man's highest gift, the philosophers concentrated more and more upon cool intellect as the great mark of progress, even going so far in modern days as seeking to know what knowing is, what proof is, the "meaning of meaning"—the Narcissus-like introversion of philosophy, intellect studying itself alone. Like Aristotle's God, intellect here loves only itself, it doesn't even love to contemplate reality. Don't we then need today an Agapology to take us out of this self-centered intellect, to have intellect *love being,* to realize its own value as understanding *what* is real and *why* it is real?

So then, the Agapologist, with his value-approach, is led to turn his torch toward the dark road ahead of his inquiring intellect, the darkness of the mystery of God's being—of any being at all—and brighten it up if he can. Here his opponent confronts him and declares that there is no such road; there is but a blank black wall and turning his light on it will only reveal its blackness. Wherefore he had better turn it behind him and study what has actually come to be. Yet after all is this assertion so different from what, according to the story (perhaps untrue), the priests replied to the astronomer when he declared that certain planets existed and if they looked through his telescope they would see them, "What is the use of looking? We know they aren't there"? And just as those skeptics *ought* to have looked through the telescope, so the rationalist *ought* to look at the suggestion given by the *good,* to consider if there isn't some way not yet found of solving this mystery. Yes, the *duty* to scrutinize it is there, no matter how impossible the task appears. The conscientious, clear-

minded intellect cannot honestly rest content with a mystery.
It is, he sees, a contradiction of intellect's very being to seek a
cause for the sunrise, a cause for the solar system, for the
galaxies and their movements, and so on, and then to stop
suddenly and avow that no further reason can be found.
Reason demands consistency! If the moral law of intellect is
to find always a reason why, certainly intellect cannot acquiesce in a command that bids it stop. And it is no blind faith
that urges on the thinker till he gets his final rest in the self-
evident. It is an irrefutable insight into reason itself. Whoever
refuses to see it is like the eager moralist who does the right
time after time, then finally yields to temptation, saying it is
too hard to resist. Yes, for the religious ones intellect's moral
law *demands* a solution of the mystery of God's being, of why
and how it is a necessity just in itself. And for the non-re-
ligious, the like holds for the mystery of being.

And we are moved toward this problem and its solution, as
we have been urging, by the simple everyday fact that there
is a hint, a suggestion, in the possible good moving to realize
itself when it isn't yet real, which *may* light up the road to
understand this darkest of mysteries, why God has His being,
why indeed there is any being at all rather than no being.

Come Then To The Argument!

Well, surprising as it may seem, we shall *begin* by proceeding along the road, not by viewing it in the light of the value-
aspect, but by the guidance of the very notion which seems so
utterly different therefrom—chance. We did notice above that
the definitions of love and chance are very much alike. But
now, moving by the lead of the meaning of chance, we shall
come to see that it is an apriori principle solving our mystery
and in so doing it reveals its identity with love. So we begin
by studying the significance of chance.

CHAPTER IV

THE ONTOLOGICAL PROOF

The Significance Of Chance: Some Objections Met

Notice that the objections to our view of evolution in Chapter II turned on the claim that the mutations were chance-events. And you might think that the view we defended goes against that. If, as we claimed, there was a persisting trend in life from its beginning toward more and more good things, as it were a *law* of life, how could this be a matter of just chance? Yet, on the contrary, we do accept the statement: the mutations were chance-events. And so far from denying the above law of progress, this confirms it. All depends on recognizing the proper meaning of chance. Because of the importance of that meaning, let us repeat what we said above about it.

To the scientist of the 19th century, chance spelled ignorance. A chance-event was *only* one whose cause we hadn't yet discovered. The orthodox teaching was a rigid determinism. But that is not the case today. Chance is in better repute. The scientist is more open-minded than he used to be. After all, doesn't rigid determinism savor of the austere puritan morality now so largely gone by? Striking it is that the science of physics, most nearly precise of the sciences in its measurements and predictions, formerly considered *the* exact science, was the first to welcome its one-time foe as a friend in its concept of statistical law. True, some of our physicists haven't so done—Planck, Einstein, for instance. These have still stood for a rigid determinism, though they admit it isn't yet proved.

But for the majority who do accept the reality of chance, the significance of it lies in this, that chance is not at all a negative thing, ignorance, rather it is a positive principle. Nor does it mean that *anything* may happen, no telling what. It means that *everything* within the limits dictated by the particular law *will* happen as time goes on.

See then the basic character of this notion. Why can't we say that each particular event which occurs within the limits dictated by a statistical law *may* be strictly determined by other laws? Because of just one trait: such determination couldn't account for the fact that all the possible cases are just about equally realized in number. Mere causal determination isn't enough. There is another principle at work: the principle of *equal* realization of all alike. Perhaps we may sense something of the significance of this principle if we note its analogy to the political doctrine of Democracy. For a powerful monarchy, as in the old days, the ruler prescribes what the individual can do and what he must do. It looks something like rigid law. For an ideal Democracy, on the other hand, there is equal *opportunity* for each individual to realize his own potentialities to the full, no conflicts between individuals. It is the note of equality that stands out. Give everyone his chance! And also note this in the nature of statistical law—we shall later see its significance—there is something of a *timeless* quality in its chance-variations. The present variation is not determined by the one just preceding it. If in tossing coins there has occurred for a while a surplus of heads over tails, all we can say is that sooner or later this will be balanced by a surplus of tails; but *when* that will come is not determined. No particular past event in the series determines any present or future event. It is as if the principle of balance were equally present, unchanging all through the series, unaffected by time, so far timeless.

But now of course comes an objection which indeed we might have considered earlier, an objection especially pertinent in regard to our "ontological" argument to come, based as that will be on the acceptance of chance in the way here defined. It is the determinist who now speaks. For everything that is, he declares, there must be a reason why, a cause. Reason demands it! And when we find the cause, as so often we do, reason is satisfied, at rest. On the other hand, as chance gives no cause for this or that particular variation, it frustrates reason, reason just cannot admit it, however strong seems to be the empirical evidence which has convinced so many of our scientists. Chance is irrational, reason which we all do respect *must* follow a rigid determinism.

Well, the answer we now give shows, on the contrary, that this determinism *fails* to explain what it claims to explain. Really it is but a *sham* explanation, a pretence to do what it doesn't do, can't do.

Determinism A Sham Rationalism

Here is an event, let us call it z—you will soon see why we use this letter! Then you discover its cause, y—and so far you look to be right. Always, wherever and whenever y occurs, it is followed by z: reason's demand is satisfied. But now look further. *Why* does y give rise to z? Because, you say, it is the very nature of y to do so. But why this nature and its existence in y? Y can't *just by itself alone* be the cause of z—if that were so, y would so far act independently, have no cause, it would be a First Cause, which as we shall see determinism doesn't permit. So we must ask: why is there y? And the only answer is, because it was caused by a previous event x. Well then, it is not y that caused z; it was x that caused y to be, and to be of such a nature that it *must* cause z. So the real cause of z is not y but x. And precisely the same applies to x. Why does x give rise to y with y's causal power? There must be a cause for this. All right, there is: we discover it when we find w, the cause of x. No, x isn't the cause of y and the z that follows y. It is w that is the cause, the reason why x behaves as it does; that behavior is thrust upon it by w; x, y, and z are but the *effects* due to w. And as you will now see, the like holds of w also; it isn't the cause of what follows it. It is but the effect of the cause v which gave rise to it. And so on without end. As we go back in the events designated by the above letters of the alphabet, there is no a, no first cause of what follows! In short, you never can find the cause which your determinism postulates. You cannot empirically verify the determinism you are defending. And as every scientific principle *must* be empirically verified, your principle of rigid determinism has no scientific justification. It isn't merely that you *don't* find the cause of the whole endless series; you can't find it. Rigid determinism is unscientific.

But perhaps the determinist will put the matter in another way. It isn't, he might say, at all a business of an endless series. It is something verified, at least to a high degree, here and now. It is the discovery of a *law*, of many different laws. *Whenever* an event of the kind x occurs, it is followed by an event of the sort y, provided nothing interferes. This is verified again and again, it is the evidence of *law: always x is the cause of y*, reason's demand for a cause, a reason why, is fulfilled. The reason why x gives rise to y isn't in x itself, rather in the *law* that it must do so. And as science advances we discover more and more laws, hence we cannot but believe that if we knew *all* about the real world we would see why everything that occurs is strictly determined: it is due to the *fact* that laws are everywhere present. Surely this is in accord with good scientific method, as we *verify* more and more laws.

Well, of course we might answer by pointing to the increasing verification today of chance in the statistical laws. Yet quite apart from this there is a point which the appeal to law, even were it strictly, perfectly verified, doesn't meet. Why this law, that law? And if you find a cause for any one law, why that cause? Some further cause must be found—and where could you stop? No, the determinist, never finding a true cause, can only *declare* the perfect rationality of the causal principles, respecting reason as we must if we are thoughtful, and the impossibility of our believing in anything having no cause, in a First Cause itself uncaused. And this drives us back to the above answer to the determinist: the series of what we call causes never gives us a cause, since every alleged cause in the series is not at all a cause but *only* the effect of some preceding event.

As a matter of fact, we shall come to see that reason's answer to the question *why* isn't confined to the realm of causing with its temporal character but is finally found in the *timeless* arena wherein dwells—as we suggested above—the principle of chance as now understood. But of course we are not here denying the presence of causal laws. We are only seeing that they don't by themselves alone account for what is.

Yet there is still another way of stating the determinist claim, as put forth by Professor Brand Blanshard in his most thorough examination and defense of it yet given, *The Nature of Thought* (London, George Allen and Unwin, 1939). As there defended, determinism means that the realm of reality *as a whole* is an organic unity, each part, element, being, event, implying all the others by strict necessity. True indeed, and rightly, he acknowledges that we limited human beings can never quite verify this empirically, as the whole of reality is too vast and complex for us to cover it completely. But not only does our steadily increasing discovery of causal laws, as in the sciences, lead to this claim about the Whole; it is an unavoidable demand of reason. Indeed, this claim of *total* organic unity does look quite to avoid the need of an uncaused cause, since not only does each part, element, group, imply the others; they in turn imply these. The implication is mutual throughout, there is no need to go further. So this view seems to avoid the first answer we gave above, claiming as we did that the search for any cause must be endless. All causes, could we survey the whole universe, physical, mental, good, bad, whatever, are for it at hand. Surely this is the best defense of determinism yet put forth!

All the same, look at some things about our universe. See for instance its general physical make-up. It is in a three-dimensional space. Why then not a four-dimensional space? Again, as a whole, including the mental, physical, good and bad, or whatever, it is temporal. Why then time? In short, take the total system and ask why this kind of a whole? To be sure, given the system, all its details can, let us for argument's sake admit, be explained by the mutual implication throughout. But whence this particular whole, *this* system? Whence the particular causal laws which reveal the mutual implication? Indeed, why any universe at all rather than nothing? No, even if we could comprehend the whole and see the organic unity in all detail, even then the demand of reason wouldn't be quite fulfilled. We must still ask why *this* whole, why any system at all, why being rather than nothing? There must be a cause, and for the determinist this must have a cause, and so on without end. Yes, after all we are back in the first difficulty—an endless search for what we can never find. Even if you can prove that this universe was caused by a perfect Creator, God, you must still ask: whence the being of God?

In fact, doesn't it now appear that there is one fundamental slip, one basic omission, at the bottom of all arguments for a complete determinism. Our criticism has turned on the nature of its causal principle. That principle would explain completely the being and nature of this or that fact, and we noted that no one single fact or event could do this of and by *itself*.

Doesn't this mean that the *individuality* of any discovered cause is lost? It does nothing of itself. Its existence as an individual vanishes into that of some other individual, its cause, and the latter again vanishes in like manner. Really, there would be no individuals in the world! Do you answer: but we see, observe, verify constantly one individual after another? But for the determinist it has no power *of just its own,* no being of itself as *merely* itself; its being vanishes into the being of its cause, and so on forever. How then can we value an individual person *just in himself,* apart from all others though not denying the values of all the others? He isn't anything but a *product* of his cause, nothing in himself. In short, how can we do what the love-gospel dictates, that brotherly love which values each for himself?

Of course, as we have said, we are to show that this love is perfectly rational. But that will mean that reason demands something more than causality, something in addition, not denying its presence but seeing in the nature of chance that which permits causal law as well as something more. So let us now return to the treatment of chance, its implications, possible objections and answers thereto.

Return To Chance

See now how chance applies to the biological mutations. As they are chance-events, shouldn't we say: the law of life, which is that living beings tend to continue their life by their reactions to the forces in the world about them, realizes itself in all possible ways, by all possible reactions in the long run? It looks so. Here comes to light one great difference between the laws of the non-living and this law of life. The former are not very far from strict repetition. Their repeated events show very minute variations, as physical science has found. But the mutations in the course of reproduction in living things, though minute in themselves, have led through the ages to a far greater breadth of variation in the latter. We know that because these variations have actually produced the vast difference between the Protista and man—such is the long road of evolution. True of course, these variations were often destructive; the trend to self-preservation was frustrated by something in the environment, some law of the inorganic perhaps, as for instance a mutation which led the animal to eat the wrong food, the poison which by the laws of chemistry paralyzed his organism. That doesn't mean that the law of self-preservation didn't hold, any more than it means the denial of the law of gravitation when an arrow is shot up in the air. The trend to preserve life is there; evolution shows it; and to preserve life, it seems, by trying all possible mutations permitted by the laws of material beings. Life is, so to speak, an experiment in self-increasing, in progress: try all possible ways to secure it!

An Objection Met

You might here object that we are wrong in calling the mutations chance-events. They are not, you say; they are caused by the laws of physics discovered of late. The proof of this lies in the fact, revealed by recent experiments of the biologist, that we can bring about mutations by X-rays acting on the parent organism. And this objection would seem to fit the doctrine of the strict determinist, every event wholly caused, no chance at all. But the evidence here given doesn't hold, and for two reasons. The fact that we can cause mutations doesn't in the least deny that they can and do, if not interfered with, happen by chance. In the example above of the tossed coins, we can certainly cause any of the events. Given six coins, we can take them one by one in our fingers and place them with three heads and three tails up, or all heads, or all tails, or any other combination we please. That doesn't show that if we let them fall as they will there is no chance present. So with the living mutations, if we don't interfere they occur by chance. And secondly, the causal laws to which the objection appeals are themselves statistical laws. *Their* events vary by chance, within minute limits. It is then surely necessary that even those laws would give rise to mutations by chance, due to the chance-variations in the laws of the inorganic themselves, if to no other source.

So we can meet the objection that a machine might be constructed which would shoot out one dime-coin after another so accurately that each would land head up. And the more nearly perfect the machine, the more certain this result. The actual occurrence of chance variations when *we* with our varying movements toss the coin is then simply due to the failure of exact repetition in those tossing movements of ours. Of course the answer is obvious. Even the most nearly perfect machine, giving the result with all heads up, would land each coin at a slightly different angle from some others, not all being perfectly parallel to the plane whereon they land. And why? Because, as the physicists tell us, the laws of the inorganic are statistical laws. No law is exactly, precisely fulfilled in the series of events—not even the law of gravitation. Even the machine just mentioned couldn't possibly behave *precisely* the same in every toss it made. True indeed, the degree of variation may be diminished as the machine is made more and more approaching perfection—and you might think this points to a rigid determination as the limit approached. But this limit is never reached, never can be reached, since all these laws are statistical.

So it is the doctrine of chance which shows us *why* life was bound to give rise to conscious mind and its values, goods. It is just because chance means all possible variations that these latest forms *must* come sooner or later when there is nothing interfering. Yes, without the modern discovery of the statistical nature of laws, evolution would seem quite unaccountable.

Thus it was that the nature of life, even in the lowest and simplest forms, to continue itself, opened the gate and pushed those forms with their power to reproduce—itself a way of continuing life—along toward the maximum possible of life, the final step so far: realization of life as *good,* as something that *ought* to be cherished and promoted. Maximum, we say, and why? Because by the inheritance given in reproduction the earlier gains tend to persist, and the successful new mutations are added to them. Evolution is additive, a process in the long run of increase. That is why it has been called emergent evolution. Of course, as we have noted, there have been backward ones, destructive of life. But also of course when all possible mutations are bound to occur the successful ones will prolong life and will open the door to all possible new mutations. And since the ones which brought in conscious mind and intelligence and the felt lure of the good were on the whole the fullest realization yet given of life's law, we may say that this law *means* the realization of the good. Evolution is itself the self-realizing of the good, due to the chance-motive, so to speak, at its very center.

A Deeper Objection

But now comes another objection. Perhaps this alleged law of chance, so to call it, does explain why the good is self-realizing. But we haven't explained why there is this chance. Why should chance come on the scene rather than rigid law? Or why this kind of chance rather than the kind which means that anything whatever may happen, no law of any sort at all? We said this approach to the mystery of self-existence would explain the mystery, but the mystery is only put off, for why is there this chance we have appealed to?

Yes, the objector has a point here. But as we said, this matter of chance is only an approach, an introduction to the argument to come. Let the objector wait until we give that. It

will show that chance is an apriori logical necessity! It has a
proof which determinism can't give.

A Problem For Philosophy

Yet there is a special difficulty in the relation of life to the
non-living which has led to conflicting views, at least among
the philosophers. We want a consistent account of things. We
want to see how the above law of life fits in with the laws of
the non-living. Well now, is there any conceivable combination, or variation even by chance, of the non-living particles
or waves which could give rise to this peculiar trait of life,
its conscious mind? When mind enters the scene with its
goods and bads, its values, there looks to be a great gulf between it and the physical. There is nothing of these values in
matter as just matter; there are no values in the inorganic
just by itself, no *feelings*. How utterly impossible then it is
to see how there could come to be in the non-living world
which preceded life, any chance-variation which would produce mind. There appears a discrepancy, an inconsistency
here. It is the old dualism of mind and body, stressed deeply
by Descartes. Hence the scientifically inclined philosopher feels
driven to deny this dualism, to defend materialism. And the
more religiously inclined thinker turns to idealism. Surely
reality must be one consistent system!

But now witness something about material things.

Your Body Feels

Admit we may that apart from life a body can't be conscious, isn't conscious even in the living plants. Yet conscious
life here on earth is always *in* a physical body, matter. Matter
so far *does* contain mind and its goods; there can be nothing
in its nature to forbid, prevent, the entry of these in the course
of evolution. After all, in everyday life it is our *bodies* that
feel good or bad. Feeling, you say, is just a mental fact. Yes,

but it isn't merely mental when you have a headache or enjoy
the taste of your food. It is your *skin* that itches, your *legs*
that feel tired. True, there is much about the body which
inhibits mental processes, as when you are tired and fall into
a dreamless sleep, or are knocked unconscious by a blow. Yet
there is also in our bodies when they are strong and well a
help to clear thinking as well as to good feeling. Our philosophers, idealist or materialist, don't realize that the body *itself*
feels, *itself* is conscious and *senses* values. No, we cannot say
that there is a gap, a gulf between body and mind. Still less
can we declare that their difference, obvious and important
as it is, rules out their unity, is even hostile thereto. It is just
straight fact that as evolution has gone on the living *body*
with its growing conscious mind has come to contain more
and more *felt* goods—greater length of life, finer tastes, greater
joys in seeing and hearing *with eye and ear* as in travel, painting, music and other arts which primitive man scarcely knew.
May we here remind the pious Christian, so often inclined to
disvalue the fleshly body, that Jesus never said the flesh contains no good; he said only that it is weak. Christianity has
all along taught that he saved his *body* in the resurrection.
Certainly he approved of the joys of the flesh: he cured disease, gave food to the multitude, turned water into wine. Have
our good Christians appreciated the fact that his last loving
meeting with his disciples was a *meal,* with its joyous food
and wine? However much there is in the physique of man
which is blind to the nobler impulses, the goods of unselfish
devotion, brotherly love, and such, these goods *have* been
realized to a high degree by *bodily* works, exercise of the
muscles, and the brain too. When the apostle James said
"faith without works is dead" he was stressing the part our
bodies should play. No, the body needn't be always the enemy
of the spirit; on the contrary, it is a necessary agent in the
emergence of more and more of that supreme virtue *love,*

which implies bodily work for our fellows. Yes, even thought, that most ethereal, immaterial function, goes with the *matter* of the brain, emotion with the autonomic nervous system, action with the efferent nervous system leading out to the muscles. And as all these must play their part in the developing of the moral good, surely there must be something in the very nature of matter which contributes to that greatest of goods. Read the book by H. Saxton Burr: *The Nature of Man and the Meaning of Existence* (C. C. Thomas, Springfield, Illinois, 1962) which confirms this by straight scientific evidence. True, the above doesn't yet tell us why or how life came to be lodged in material things; it is but an introduction to the solution of that problem, though a helpful, even a necessary one as we shall see.

How Matter Can Become Conscious

See now that even this non-living material world is really not so utterly different from the mental realm as most have believed. Here witness the progress of physical science, as stated by Henry Margenau (*Open Vistas,* Yale Univ. Press, 1960, pp. 126-7): "is everything that exists material? A simple but perfectly proper answer would be: matter is no longer material in spite of the literal contradiction in terms. But since the ultimate constituents of matter have resolved themselves pretty much into mathematical singularities haunting space, materialism is no longer the comfortable doctrine it used to be, and one may dismiss it as having lost its major point." Of course, mere "mathematical" things as just equations, formulas, are not real; their reality lies in their "singularity", their individual being as events in space-time—which means as instances of energy, of power giving rise to further events. The point is: the old view of matter as solid inert *stuff,* incapable of doing anything unless laws are added to it—this view has gone, vanished. Certainly nothing could be so different from spirit, from conscious mind, as such an inert stuff. On the other hand, productive energy is to a degree analogous to our mental experience of doing, of activity. It need not be conscious, but it has that latent within it which *can* become conscious. Inert dead stuff cannot become conscious, since it is wholly confined to its own passive being, whereas consciousness goes beyond the individual possessing it to include in its mind some object other than that individual alone. But when matter is seen to be energy it does contain, every bit of it contains, an implication of a possible something besides itself. True, that something is a future event, and so far is a separate being from the present one. That is the nature of time: the future is not present, it is separated from the present, not at all actual then and there. But in energy it is potentially present, there is an implicit connection with the present. Just because of this implicit connection with the future, this present energy may *become* conscious. Consciousness is the mental realization at the present moment, the *explicit* presence, of what without it is *only* potential, implicit. The conscious mind is *aware* of the possible future, that possible future is explicitly *present* to the conscious mind. So we can see how the very nature of material being as revealed of late by our scientists makes possible the entrance of conscious mind. We couldn't see that when we thought of matter as purely passive solid stuff, each bit just its inert individual being, no more. Yes, it is the very nature of material being, as physical science has shown, that consciousness *may* develop in it.

Of course this doesn't mean that consciousness is at all present in all material things, as the idealists have claimed. Unconscious bodies are just as real as conscious bodies. Consciousness isn't *lurking* in the non-living world. That world is so made that it may *begin* to lurk therein, as in the advent of primitive life before minds came on the scene. But we can't point to any *compulsion* in the laws of the non-living that life and mind will appear. That event is due, as we found in Chapter II, to the agency of chance as seen in the course of evolution.

See then how significant all this is for the possible future of conscious minds on this material earth. It brings to light the potentialities of their living bodies as the old view of the *wholly exclusive* mind-body dualism couldn't suggest. Not that the mind-body dualism is overcome, denied. No, it is real. It is the *necessary* exclusiveness between the two, spirit and flesh, which the view here presented denies. The nature of body as body remains in space and time, and body as being such is *so far* not at all mind, being unconscious. But inasmuch as its make-up is energy, productive activity, body and mind *may* come to unite more and more. Certainly we must reject the Cartesian exclusion, even hostility, between the two.

Yes, this explains why, as we said, our bodies can be and are good in themselves—when they *feel* good to us. The joys of eating, drinking, physical exercise, rest, these are, if the stern moralist could see it, just *good*. If sometimes they interfere with other goods, as with the sensualist who cares for little else, it is the interference which is bad. The flesh is, can be, divinely joyous, embodying more and more spirit-goods.

And all this is further confirmed by recent biological evidence, which shows that evolution isn't only something which started ages ago but has been and is continually starting, now as in the past. See the work by A. I. Oparin, *The Origin of Life,* 1957. This biologist says that the readiness of the inorganic materials for the entrance of life and mind is just as much present today as ever; it is inherent in the nature of non-living matter, at least on this earth. Witness the viruses, lowest forms of life so far known. It is scarcely credible that they arose only at the beginning of evolution and have continued ever since in the same simple make-up. And the like holds of the now living bacteria with their enormous numbers.

How could these remain the same as when they first arose, with little or no variation through the long ages? Surely they have been and are still originating as time goes on. Yes, the chemical combinations which open the gate to life are inherent in matter, go on continually; there is something in the very nature of matter which will always give life and mind their opportunity. No wonder that our bodies *themselves* feel! Such is the testimony of what the biologists call by the highly technical term "repetitive neobiogenesis".

Chance, we affirm then, has been and still is a mighty agent in the long history of our world from earliest non-living ages to the advent of life and its evolution. It was not alone, of course; doubtless there were always nature's laws—statistical laws to be sure. Note in passing that a highly respected philosopher, A. N. Whitehead, has claimed that these laws themselves change and evolve. But anyway the fact of progress, of emergence to higher levels, to the presence of values at last, and increasing values too, is clearly due, not to the laws as rigidly determining, but to the principle of random variation, small indeed in life and in the non-living, but increasingly productive as time goes on in life.

We put the question above: why this agent, chance? And we promised to answer it, to show that chance as now understood is an apriori logical necessity. That, we declare, is the road by which we can solve the old puzzle, the mystery of being, and thereby the mystery of God's self-existence, and why the good realizes itself perfectly in Him, and in His creatures in their limited and analogous way. And this realization which is perfect in Him is, we shall see, the very essence of love. Hence, our title *Agapology!* But now comes an objection by the strict rationalist.

Is Chance A Proved Fact?

You may say that is not proved beyond any possible doubt.

It is never *completely* verified. You may toss your coins for just an hour, and find that the combinations which have come up do fulfill *precisely* what the principle of chance dictates— all possible ones realized in just the proportion which their head-tail ratio permits. But if you go on tossing, the new tosses will show a variation—perhaps more cases of all heads, or of all tails, or of this or that combination, than the law declares. True, these will be counterbalanced again sometime, but even then if the process continues, variations will come up. We might answer: nevertheless in the long run the combinations will verify the principle of equal realization. Well, how long is the long run? As far as possible human experimenting can go, it is never ended. Chance as here defined is never *quite* fulfilled. Is it indeed any more nearly verified than the evidence for determinism in nature's causal laws? No, it isn't *proved* to be a real principle. If as our scientists have come to see, strict causal law isn't precisely proved, neither is chance as a factor in statistical laws. Isn't that why some of our top scientists such as Einstein and Planck have still believed in rigid determinism?

Yes, there is indeed a point here. With our present knowledge due to the very, very careful empirical work of the scientist, neither is proved. At the same time there is a suggestion which we can't just dismiss. To repeat, we can't overlook even in our statistical laws the on-the-whole regularities in nature's ways, and equally we can't deny the *approximate* verification, time and again, of the fact of *equality* in the variations. It certainly looks *as if* there were in addition to the regularity another principle at work. True indeed, up to this stage of our argument we have simply assumed as a working hypothesis, so to speak, that this second principle, which after all is just as *near* to being empirically confirmed as its rival, is true. But soon we shall give what we claim to be a strict proof of its reality.

Even now we may give a hint in that direction. There *is* something in the nature of chance which seems to suggest, to point toward, the trait of logical necessity. We noted above a certain timeless quality in it: no one variation determined by the particular one preceding it, by any one preceding it. It is as if the *whole* series with its note of equality in the variations were somehow present, presiding over the individual variations as they occur in time. Well, isn't a pure straight logical necessity quite timeless? Such is the case with the necessary truths of arithemetic, algebra, geometry—of mathematics generally. Doesn't this timeless quality in chance suggest that it may be somehow connected with an apriori logical necessity? However, we leave this in the air for the present.

In the air, yes; for we have all along been walking on the solid ground of fact, of being, and what right have we, what possibility have we, to go anywhere except by treading this road? Look again at our argument in Chapter II about the good realizing itself. As we have admitted above, how could it realize itself unless there were already there beings in whom it could do so? Even our notion of chance we got from empirical observation of real things by the scientist, of the actual events in statistical laws, tossing coins, dice, and such. How could there be any principle at all, still less apriori, unless it applied to beings? Away with this notion of apriori necessity, there can't be any such thing! Even in your alleged timeless apriori truths of arithmetic, didn't they come to your mind only after you had come to *count* real things?

So now for our central pivotal thesis: we *can* go out beyond the realm we have so far traversed. And the evidence that we can will show that being itself, God Himself, is due to chance as apriori necessary—chance of course as here defined, not in the old sense that anything might happen to be or not to be.

It will be helpful here to begin by tracing a certain phase of the recent growth of intellect in mankind. It will lead us to see something implied by reason itself which we haven't yet brought out.

Looking Behind Being

Man early began looking for the causes of things. He had to know something of the future in order to conduct his life with success; to know that, he must discover the regular sequences of events in the world. He must be able to predict what would cause what, to know nature's laws. Thus originated man's interest in finding out those laws, from a *practical* motive. And as his evolution went on, he came at length to see the *beauty* of law: law is order, system, every event accounted for. The rational motive now took the chair, presided over his thinking. So satisfactory, so beautiful is law and order that he comes to believe everything must have it. Reason becomes his god; reason is the finding of reasons for everything that is. So utterly gratifying is this conviction that he carries his search for reasons out into the starry universe, inward into the realm of his body and mind itself. So originated the empirical sciences: astronomy, physics, chemistry, biology, psychology. And alongside these came the *purely* rational science, mathematics; purely rational we say, because of its detachment more and more from the observation of actual events in the world to ideal systems deduced by reason from postulated axioms. Here the practical motive evaporated, as it never quite did in the empirical sciences; though even in these the main urge came to be love of knowledge for its own sake. But it was for them knowledge of fact first, explanation by causal law the grace, the glorifying crown of that knowledge.

Such was the gradual process of man's intellectual evolution: a well-nigh exclusive devotion to reason as the supreme principle of reality, even of the human mind. It was most exampled in the Greeks with their philosophers, notably Aristotle, and mathematicians, notably Euclid. Their influence pervaded Western civilization more and more, extolling intellect when biological evolution was discovered, as man's highest faculty. The natural result was the extraordinary development of the sciences up to recent times—law everywhere, everything strictly determined, no possible events except those which have occurred and will occur. The possible is the real to come in this given universe, nothing else, nothing more.

Then came forth the latest stage, giving the notion of possibility as something worth studying by itself, something beyond the region of actual things. And it came, strangely enough, through the door of that most purely rational pursuit, mathematics. This branch of science, really a science quite alone by itself, is not empirical, not concerned with reality; it works by logical implication alone. Here reason is, so to say, dwelling in its own house, isolated from the realm of fact, of being. It tells us, and it tells us, notice, from the standpoint of pure reason, that being itself implies its complement, its counterpart, possibility—*what might be but isn't*. We might say in metaphor that reason shuts the door leading to the outer world and looks up through the skylight into empty space above, where it sees glimmering lights here and there, quite afar from the solid ground of reality on which its own house was built.

A mathematical system begins with certain axioms from which it deduces by strict reasoning the rest of the system. What does the word *axiom* mean? It is derived from the Greek word meaning "to deem worthy". It was in the past so deemed by the intellect because it seemed self-evident, self-justifying quite by itself, worthy of reason's respect. So it was with the axioms of Euclidean geometry. To its founder they looked self-evident. And so they are, in our three-dimensional world as perceived by our senses. See then, there is an accidental element here. It is for *reason* no matter of necessity.

If it were, no other axioms would be intelligible. But the modern mathematician, devotee of pure reason, sees easily that other axioms *might* be, are *possibles,* though not in this world. Actually we are living in a three-dimensional space— at least it looks so. But why not a four-dimensional, five, six, or any number of dimensions? No apriori necessity can be found in our present Euclidean axioms. As the devout Christian might say, God chose freely to make our world as it is, no logical compulsion about it. He could have created a very different world. The Euclidean axioms are not a whit more self-evident in themselves than many others which the mathematicians have proposed in their systems of hypergeometry. Nor are any of these others dictated by necessity, they are just possibles quite apart from this real world. Hence they are now no longer called axioms, as if self-justifying, but postulates. So there has emerged into view a realm of possibles such as was never thought of before. Even further, as we shall see in a moment, this realm is so vast that we cannot but consider it infinite. And from all this we learn that whatever is, is just a possible, a group of possibles, which is realized. *All being is derived from possibles!* Logically speaking, possibles precede being, nothing can be unless it was first possible. But this word "first" is here not to be taken in a temporal sense. The possibles we are now considering are timeless.

Yes, only when the race of mathematicians came to devote themselves to the realm of pure logical implication quite apart from being, as with Bolyai, Lobatchewsky, and many others, did they see that no particular geometrical axioms are self-evident alone, none more worthy to be, more necessary apriori, than any others. So opened itself to them the *separate* realm of possibles, and mathematics became the science of possibles and deductions from them by pure reason.

It is intellect itself, just by itself, which has revealed to us this region of possibles. Oh no, you may object, it isn't intellect at all, it is only imagination. We can imagine all sorts of things that aren't real, even couldn't be real: a phoenix, a red-haired oyster, a round square. True indeed, we answer, with respect to *our actual* world. But imagination doesn't by itself raise the question of possible being. It is only the presence of an idea, whether that idea could be actual in some other kind of world is another matter. So man invents fairy stories. Reflection, thought, is what considers whether or not they could be real; it is observation which verifies or denies their possibility in this world. Without imagination, to be sure, intellect couldn't conceive of possibles; ideas are the material with which it works. The greater the scientist, the mathematician, the more imagination must he have. But intellect alone can tell us whether an idea, notion, or proposition is neither self-contradictory nor conflicting with any apriori necessity. And if it is neither of these it is surely a possibility, it might have been real in a created world different from ours, though it can't be so here. Notice by the way that intellect has revealed to us two regions of possibles—we must not confuse them. There are things, events, which are possible in this temporal world though not actual here and now. Such are those which belong to the process of statistical laws. Any one of the minute variations may happen at some time, all will happen sooner or later. Even the determinist who denies these possibles has his own kind of possibles: what is bound to happen in the future. Of course in this given temporal world there are plenty of impossibles: centaurs, round squares, innumerable others. The possibles we have just named, however, are temporal possibles, in the future, determined or not. But the mathematician has brought to light a very different arena of possibles not of this world, not a matter of its future, timeless possibles they are. We shall here call them ultimate possibles. Indeed, even these ultimate possibles do include not only other kinds of things than those of this universe; they include the latter too. Our universe had to be possible, since it does exist. Its possibles and realities are only certain particular ultimate possibles made real, excluding all others, in our given space-time universe.

Well, we are now to see how this discovery of ultimate possibles brings forth a contribution by intellect such as no empirical science, no study of reality alone, can offer; a gift which is obviously available in the value-realm and will, incredible as it may seem, verify our thesis that the good is self-realizing by explaining why it *must* be so.

But here pause a moment and reflect: what is this arena of timeless possibles? It surely looks queer! Where is it? How can there *be* such a realm? If we look at the metaphysical systems of the past we don't learn much about it, and naturally so, since metaphysics was taken—and rightly so far—as the study of reality. Let us then look again at its nature, its meaning, its extent.

The Drawing Expanse Of Timeless Ultimate Possibles

We repeat: how did the mathematician come to conceive of these possibles? Remember: his ruling motive, his loving pursuit, was and is exact irrefutable proof. He loves logical necessity, it is his final good. He doesn't care much about facts, reality. He longs for rigid demonstration for its own sake. The physicist does too, so he uses mathematics greatly; but he has an even greater interest in beings, events. Notice then: the mathematician, loving logical necessity for itself, asks "What *follows* from this or that, from any notion, proposition, whatever?" He sees that what is actual around him doesn't follow from anything but some other actual, he feels that not its actual being but its following is the interesting thing. It is this motive which alone guides him: anything to give me logical necessity, whether about real things or not! So he conjures up all sorts of possibles—notions not self-contradicting—

to see what would follow from them. And this suggests to us the onlookers that such a realm of possibles is far greater than what his hypergeometries reveal—as we noted above. If we look at the physical laws which goven this world, we see no logical necessity for just these laws. Why is there electric attraction and repulsion? Why light-waves? Why gravitation? There is no apriori necessity for these rather than other laws. An ingenious mind can think up many others that might have ruled our universe. Is there any limit to these possibles? As the religious one might say: God could have created any number of worlds, universes, with laws quite different from these we find here. But more than this, we spoke only of the inorganic world. Once our intellect is roused to see these indefinitely vast physical possibilities, we can see the like in the realm of conscious life, of values. Are there not many, many possible goods which we cannot yet think of, even goods not possible for our limited human biology and psychology? Think how the goods of our human life have increased since the evolution of mankind began, increased both in degree and kind. Is there any limit to the possible goods. If there is, we cannot find it. So dawns upon the thinker the notion of perfection, perfection the realization of all ultimately possible goods. And to the religious urge deep within our hearts there enters the idea of a Perfect Being. No longer can the many gods satisfy the intelligent mind, with the limited goods in each; the highest good conceivable would be One Supreme Being Who realized all possible goods in Himself. Perhaps that is why, as human history went on, mankind as it grew more thoughtful turned gradually away from polytheism to monotheism. A being who could embody *all* the possible goods in His one person is far more to be revered and worshipped than any number of more or less imperfect gods. He is the Supreme Ideal. He contains within His own single being all possible power, knowledge, goodness. Being all-powerful, He might create any of those

hypergeometry worlds which the mathematicians have discovered, or any world whatever which is conceivable—conceivable to His perfect intellect, not confined to what we
finite intellects find conceivable. "With God all things are
possible." And of course, as Anselm felt but didn't quite prove
(see Chapter III), If He is perfect He must have the power
to *be,* He must be self-existent. Such then is the vast, the limitless extent of the realm of timeless possibles which gradually
dawns on us.

To be sure, our modern religions didn't originate in the
above way; they came as proclaimed by prophets, as revelations from on high. We are but giving as it were a justification
of their appeal to their fellows. True also, this idea of perfection dawned on men's minds long before the mathematicians thought of possible realms not realized in our world.
Why then? Because it was in the realm of values, goods for
which human nature longs, and that craving for goods, basic
in conscious mind, is present long before intellect is highly
developed. But we can see now how it fits into the pattern of
intellect's latest visions, and enlarges them as if without limit.

Yet so far we have been speaking only of the *idea* of all
possible goods being realized in One Being. So far as we have
here treated the matter, it is only that this *idea* came to commend itself at length to the thoughtful religious mind, and of
late the work of the mathematicians has given it some *suggestion* of a rational basis. It is our emotional life, our value-
phase, which warms our hearts to believe in this Being Who
is Himself all that being could possibly be, no limitation whatever. And as the good looks to be the highest, richest form of
being, we conceive of Him as perfect, perfection the realization, the *existence* of all possible goods, none left alone outside
Him, and no mere possibles within Him, as all are fulfilled in
His being. And further, since we have seen that the good, even
this or that little good in our human lives, tends to realize it-

self, then perhaps the supreme goodness of our God will realize itself in the spirit-world where is no matter, no physical law to interfere—as we suggested at the end of Chapter II.

Grant all this if you may, yet it is so far scarcely more than wishful belief. The main point has still to be shown: why *must* the possible good be self-realizing and so far self-existent? Or to put it in the form we gave it above: *why* the principle of chance, which asserts the realization of all possibles? Come now to this. If we can answer the question about chance we can see and understand the logical necessity of God's being just by Himself, we can prove that and why there must *be* the Perfect One, quite apart from His creating this world as its logically implied cause.

The Argument's Basis

Prove, we said. But proof is for the intellect to find. And intellect concerning itself with being, has two and only two motives. It would know *what* is and *why* it is. Its two questions are What? and Why? Never will it, never can it, finally rest content with the answer to the first alone. The scientist would discover more and more facts, yet never be satisfied until he could explain their presence. So, too, the philosopher if he truly respects reason. Intellect, like man himself, stands on two feet: the one moving forward to see *what* is, the other following up to see *why* it is. Both feet must be used or he will lose his balance! So also for the sincere religious believer. He feels, should feel, that his intellect is a gift from the loving Creator, and he should revere that gift, use it with no stopping, no hindrance. If he knows—or believes that he knows— that God exists, he must seek to know why God exists. And indeed for all thinkers alike, religious or not, the final, the ultimate question dawns: why is there any being at all rather than just nothing? Thus, we have the mystery of being. If intellect is honest with itself, it cannot turn its back on the mystery of being.

Yes, no matter how certain the worshipper is of the existence of God, the Perfect One, no matter how irrefutable is the proof that the cause of this actual universe is the Almighty God—many deny this proof today—that is never quite enough for the thoroughgoing intellect. For the causal proof itself— granting it for argument's sake—starts from the given *fact* of this universe, and ends in the *fact* of God's being. But this only answers the first of the two questions which intellect must always ask: the question *What*. It doesn't touch the second question *Why*. Why the existence of God the First Cause, why His being just by Himself? Intellect is still in the realm of being, of *What* is. It must go further, and to go further is to look behind the realm of being and ask: *Why* any being? And the only realm behind being is that realm which we have seen gradually dawning upon thoughtful minds—the arena of the possible. Being is possible of course, since it is actual; but *Why* is this possible actual? So we are led to what appears the darkest of all problems, the mystery of being. And the arena is so dark that many refuse to enter it; they see no light to guide them.

We said above that the *What* motive steps forward to new knowledge, and the *Why* motive steps up to counterbalance it, to prevent the mover from toppling over. Toppling over into what? Into the realm of mystery, mystery which is the intellect's basic evil and must be abolished! Well, the second step is due to the intellect's *inborn certainty* that there is always a reason why, and orders the searching mind to discover that reason. This certainty is what has been dubbed the Principle of Sufficent Reason. It is reason's basic apriori universal truth. And as the mystery of being cannot be solved by empirical observation, since that only gives being over again, the only possible resource at hand for solving the mystery is the above principle. Come then to see what is implied in the Principle of Sufficient Reason. And the discovery of that, which will give the solution of the mystery, we shall at length find, reveals the core and center of the Agapology metaphysic, the unity of love and reason and chance which is God Himself.

Ultimate Possibles As Self-Realizing

Let us repeat again the opposition that confronts us here; it may serve to strengthen our pursuit! Limited as our human intelligence is and must be, so many theologians have said, we couldn't possibly penetrate what only the infinite intelligence of God can understand. Yet this overlooks reason's moral law, as we saw in Chapter III and have just now stressed again. If the moral law of reason is *always* to find a reason why, we cannot acquiesce in a teaching which bids it stop anywhere on the road. It is no blind faith that urges on the thinker till he gets his final rest in the self-evident. It is an irrefutable insight into what is demanded. Even Kant who denied the ontological argument declared, "you ought, therefore you can." To repeat once more: as we saw in Chapter III, whoever refuses to see this is like the earnest moralist who does the right time after time, then finally yields to temptation, saying it is too hard to resist.

Too hard, yes? For it might be expected that a proof in this matter, absolutely ultimate as it must be, would be of the longest and most complex form conceivable—so much so as to make it impossible for us to carry it through. On the contrary, as we shall see, it is utterly simple, the very extreme of simplicity, concerned as it will be only with the notions *being, possible,* and *nothing,* each a concept of the least complexity, yet applying to the maximum area of things. *Being* applies to *anything and everything* which exists, *nothing* applies to *not anything whatsoever, possible* to all the ultimates we spoke of above and also to all that is. The most inclusive, most universal in its application, is the simplest! Ever we explain the complex by the simple—recall how we dwelt on this matter of simplicity in the Preface above.

Now then to the argument. Note that as said, though we are to treat of the ontological proof of God's being, we don't come at once to that. We begin with the mystery of being. All the same, it will be helpful to look first at some forms of that proof as hitherto proposed, and see how they have a certain defect which pushes us on to meet the mystery of being.

The Proofs Hitherto Offered

These ways of giving the ontological proof, which *should* demonstrate the apriori logical necessity of God's being, a being inevitable just by itself, not inferred from any *characters* presented in the *facts* of this world, do in fact use a notion drawn from such a character. That is the notion of perfection, which as we saw above, is drawn from *our experience* of the good, of value. That experience suggested to mankind the idea of a possible perfect good. So Anselm, seeing that this perfect good wouldn't be perfect unless it had the power to be, offered his argument. Stating it as we did above, we accepted the criticism thereof by Aquinas. Yet even if Anselm's argument were correct, that argument is not quite an apriori proof; it is drawn from a certain trait of this *actual* world, the trait of value, good. Why should there be such a trait? No reason has been given. Value is, after all, a fact, a way of being. Why then this way? Why any being at all? Yes, we must first solve the ultimate mystery, mystery of being. Then perhaps we may come to see why there must be good being, even a Perfect Being. But surely we cannot do that unless we first see why there *must* be some reality, some being. Yes, even if Anselm's argument were correct, it would not be a genuine ontological proof.

We just spoke of some other ways of putting the above argument. It is indeed a striking fact that this Anselmian offering, so long and widely rejected by Christian theologians, Catholic and Protestant alike, has recently been revived, defended, though in somewhat changed form. Doesn't that suggest that we in our hearts and minds really cannot abolish the craving for such a proof?

Well, notice first the value-form of the argument as defended by W. M. Urban, especially in his latest book *Humanity and Deity*. We don't go into the detail of his thesis, carefully worked out as it is; in fact we shall later see that his basic claim—value the ground of being—is quite true. We note only that the *fact* of value present in this world is taken as the basis of his argument, no attempt to show *why* there should present itself to us this experience of value. The mystery remains. Come now to three more examples.

As far as the present writer knows—beside his own argument given in *God and Polarity* which shall be restated and defended later—these latest ontological arguments have been given, first by two well-known and highly respected philosophers, Norman Malcolm and Charles Hartshorne. The former gave his in a twenty-three page article in the *Philosophical Review,* January 1960, the latter in a very thorough metaphysical treatise, *The Logic of Perfection and Other Essays* (Open Court Publishing Company, La Salle, Illinois, 1962). There is thirdly a brief article in the same line by the highly esteemed logician of Yale University, Professor Frederic B. Fitch, entitled "The Perfection of Perfection", *The Monist,* Spring, 1963.

Well, we are not here questioning the correctness of these new arguments as they stand. Once given the notion of perfection, from which all three start, they may be quite sound. But—we repeat—why is there this idea, this ideal of perfection, rather than no ideas at all? After all, it grew in our minds, due to something *given* in our *actual* make-up. The arguments, like Urban's, don't touch the mystery of being, however sound they are from their starting point on. And according to Professor Hartshorne this ideal is involved in the very nature of time. But why is there time? Why not a timeless world? Why any world at all? The arguments, so to speak, don't start from scratch. They rest on an empirical basis. No, we must go deeper if we want an absolute logical necessity, a proof that God must exist *no matter what*. We must see why there is *being* which can provide this ideal, can provide anything indeed. There can be no genuine proof of the apriori necessity of any particular being, perfect or not, until we explain why there is any being at all.

True, you may object, our own argument to solve the mystery of being isn't starting from scratch. We have already taken something for granted in asking the question: *why* is there being? That something is the authority of *reason*. We haven't explained why there is such a thing as reason, whence comes its authority. Isn't reason itself an actual process in our *given* human psychology, just as much so as the ideal of perfection which has dawned on our minds?

Well, there are two answers here. First, the claim we make is only to show how and why the being of anything, and particularly of God, is in complete accord with reason, an apriori logical necessity *for reason*. So far we do indeed take the authority of reason for granted—that's all we claim. We are only combating those who assert that the ground of God's being is beyond human understanding. Yes, we just *have* taken, have *assumed*—you say—without proof, the principle of sufficient reason. How could we possibly give such a proof? We are just as bad as those who start from the given ideal of perfection. So, in the second place, we answer by simply saying: the only way to prove it would be to use it in the proof. The inescapable, unavoidable *fact* is that we just can't help assuming it as absolutely right. As the distinguished mathematician Professor Cassius J. Keyser of Columbia University used to say: "you can't prove proof." Once reason dawns on your mind as self-justifying, there is finality. Of course an opponent may *refuse* to use the principle of sufficient reason beyond a certain point—nor can we compel him to change his mind—so does the existentialist philosopher today. But even he uses reason to persuade us that he is right, up to a point, where he stops and appeals to emotion alone. And of course, as we have declared, our claim is that emotion itself as seen in the love-motive, is absolutely a rational affair. No, we *can't help* respecting a *wholly* rational argument. Come then to the problem of the mystery of being.

The Simple Argument

We start with the assertion that it is an apriori necessity that there must be *either* no being at all *or* some actual being —nothing or something. Suppose than that there is being *rather than* no being at all, nothing. And when, following the principle of sufficient reason, you ask why being rather than nothing, there is no answer. The mystery remains: why any being at all? To be sure, a different answer, one which we spoke of above, has been given by Paul Weiss—we put this off for the moment, we shall consider it soon. We here only say that his answer to the mystery doesn't really disagree with the one we shall now give.

Suppose, on the other hand, that there is no being at all, just nothingness. At first that looks as if it would solve the mystery, since there is *nothing* to be explained. But the above principle asks: why nothing *rather than* something? And this answer is ruled out, because there *is* being. And yet the above either-or looks like a self-evident truth.

Here is where we meet the unique point which our philosophers and theologians don't seem to have appreciated—the crux of our whole argument, the simple tiny pivot on which it turns. Recall that we said this deepest of problems is solved by the very simplest considerations. See then: it was the *rather than,* the *either-or,* that made the failure to solve. But this either-or is not the one and only final self-evident apriori truth. It does not rule out, rather it implies, a *both-and.* Being *and* nothing can and do *both* exist side by side everywhere and always! *No explanation is needed why the one rather than the other is the case, when both are present.* The principle of sufficient reason implies the companion principle: *both* of these ultimate possibles *must* be realized. And where no explanation is needed, the mystery of being solves itself. True, you may object that *nothing* can't exist—it would be a self-contradiction. We shall answer this objection in a moment.

Yes, when we come to the mystery of being—and we might say, *only* when we do that—we see that the apriori certain principle of sufficient reason, with its *rather than,* implies another apriori necessary principle, as it were its opposite pole, the principle of *both-and*—no exclusion, no need to explain why this *rather than* that. The former principle holds within a given realm where there are exclusions—this rather than that. The counter-principle which accounts for the fact of any being at all has no exclusions, it includes *both* of the ultimate simplest possibles, being and non-being, nothing; being and beside it, nothing, both equally present. The principle of inclusion has now come into view, a self-justifying logical necessity.

We might put it this way: there are *three* alternatives when we look at the mystery of being—either-or, both-and, neither-nor. The first, we saw, implies the second, being *and* nothing. What does the third mean with its *neither* being *nor* nothing? Well, perhaps it means mere possibles, which are neither actual nor nothing at all. But then the question comes: why aren't these possibles real? A possible *may* be real, why shouldn't it be? Why unreal *rather than* real? And there is no answer, the mystery remains. Indeed, being *includes* possibles, it is the timeless realization thereof. So of the three alternatives we must say: the third gives no solution, the second is necessarily true, as it solves the problem, the first is true only if there is already a realm of being containing some exclusion, a realm which is *not*, like the above *both* being and nothing, all inclusive—again a mystery.

But what about our statement that *nothing* exists as well as something? Surely this looks like a self-contradiction. So let us now consider the point. Yes, we have indeed declared the actual presence of nothing, non-being, in reality. Well, how many philosophers or theologians have paid much attention to this concept of nothing? Except for some Existentialists who treat *nothing* as object of anxiety for a human being before the threat of death and destruction, and just one recent article in the *Review of Metaphysics,* December, 1963, by R. R. Ehman, which admits the presence of nothing, seldom has it been taken as worthy of notice—implicit as it was in some of the Oriental teaching and some Western mystical theologies. Yet we here point to an empirical verification of its presence.

Why Nothing?

Take a simple everyday commonplace example—and note its simplicity! You say to your friend who looks on your desk for a note-book he has mislaid "on my desk, as you see, are three journals and a sheet of paper, and beside them nothing." There is the testimony to the presence of nothing: we can't help speaking that way, we believe it is absolutely the truth. Non-being, nothing, can and does *accompany* being without denying it. Yes, everywhere and always it is present. Nothing is here in addition to every particular being, beside each, with each and all. Isn't it a delicious irony that in our English language the word *nowhere* is, letter by letter, the very word *now-here?* And remember, zero is a real number in arithmetic which counts real things: $1 + 2 + 3 = 6 + 0, 6 - 6 = 0$.

Let us now compare our claim, as we said we would, with that of our highly respected philosopher Paul Weiss, the only present-day thinker, so far as we know, who has dealt with the mystery of being. In his metaphysical treatise *Reality* he starts from the alternative we began with: either being or nothing. Then he affirms: of these two the second cannot exist, cannot *be,* since it would be self-contradictory that non-being could be. Hence we are by apriori logical necessity driven to the conclusion: being is the only alternative. Being is a logical necessity, the mystery is solved.

On the surface this seems to deny our claim. But it really doesn't. True indeed, nothing cannot *be* as a positive thing. Being is a positive fact. But we would here add something which Professor Weiss *could* add: there are also negative facts. The sun is not black, John Jones is not Fred Smith, and so on. And nothing, as we said, is the simplest, the universally applicable negative fact—*not anything whatsoever.* It has its own way of existing. If all fact must be positive and *only* positive, there could be only one being, not many beings, each one *not* any other one—which would deny the facts of this real world. If the simple note *being* is common to all given things, why not *also* the simple note *nothing,* present as the extreme degree of negation, that which is not, which is *other than,* all things, the simplest possible note of negation? Anyway the truth is that we just can't help but recognize it when we say this or that is here, and nothing else besides.

Oh but, you say, if nothing, non-being, is present here and now, that means that it *exists*—a self-contradiction, as Weiss said. Yes, we reply, *nothing is the one fact, the only fact, which can be self-contradictory and yet be present here and now.* Self-contradiction rules out the being of anything *except* nothing. We can admit Weiss's claim and retain the nothing. No, there is no reason for denying the *presence* of nothing, and there is every reason for asserting it, as we can't help thinking and saying that there is nothing beside what is real.

True, you might now object that the phrase "nothing else besides" doesn't mean "nothing at all". Rather it means "no things other than the ones here". As in the above example: on your desk are three journals and a sheet of paper, and no trees, no sheep, no elephants, no stars, and so on for all *other* beings than the above. Indeed you are right so far. But the above phrase *also* means "nothing at all". If you were to ask "what is there *in addition to* these given things", the answer must be "nothing at all". And that answer applies to every fact, everything throughout the real world.

Yes, we are led to the principle of *both-and* at the very basis of reality, a synthesis of polar opposites whereby each pole is just as actual *in its own way* as is the synthesis. It is inclusion which respects each element included, just for its own sake. See already how this suggests, however dimly and remotely, the notion of love between individuals, each joined with the other yet without loss of its own individuality, each respecting the individuality of the other. Such in fact is the very nature of polarity. Is that perhaps why polarity, as we saw in the book *God and Polarity,* is so fundamental a trait in the universe? At any rate, logical necessity has driven us to the wholly rational principle of *both-and,* the word *both* signifying the polar union, the word *and* signifying the distinctness of each pole.

Of course there is one more very natural objection. Of what possible use is it to dwell on this presence of nothing, even if that is the case? As it is nothing, it can't *do* anything, lead to anything, have any positive import, value, whatever. To say it is here to say nothing! And how absurd to put it as if it were on a level with being, to dub it the polar counterpart of being. Well, we are to see later that its presence with being *does* matter much in our actual world. We shall see that God, whose existence our ontological argument claims to prove, *makes use* of this nothing in the world which He creates, and for good purpose. Yet even if this weren't so, we just can't help speaking and thinking of nothing as present here and now.

Come now to the next step, the step which brings to light what we have been heading toward.

The Ontological Proof

As we said, inclusion is the keynote, *both* being and nothing, each implying the other, neither denying the other, both present side by side. Now see how this note of both-and applies to being itself. There is only one kind of nothing, just nothing at all. But there may be many kinds of being, many beings. We saw this as an ultimate possibility in the section on the dawning expanse of ultimate possibles. It then follows that every possible kind or instance of being must be realized, none to be preferred, no this *rather than* that. If some were excluded there would be a reason why, and there is no such reason. The principle of *both-and,* inclusive as it is, demands, implies by strict necessity the reality of all ultimate possibles, *none conflicting.* The situation is self-existent. And notice how this fits the meaning of chance—the realization of all possibles equally, as we have stressed above. Yes, *chance is an apriori necessity of being,* implied in the basic principle of both-and, with that principle's note of all-inclusion.

But you may ask: why *must* there be many possible kinds or instances of being? The alleged realm of ultimate possibles did, if you please, dawn on our minds; but why *should* there be such a realm? We are dealing here with apriori logical necessity, and we haven't shown that necessity in respect to *many.* Why not just one single possible instance of being and no more, nothing besides. Surely that would satisfy the both-and principle. Well, the answer is just as simple as the argument already stated. Suppose that there is apriori only one possible being, no more. Then the question comes: why just this one and no more? Why one *rather than* many? And of course there is no answer to this *rather than*. The only solution of this mystery is found, as above, in the *both-and*. So we must say: there are *both* some one particular being *and* many others. No preference of the one to the many is permitted. Nor does including the many give the many a preference over the one. The one, any one whatever, is just as present as all the many. And hereby we also see that the many cannot be limited. If they were, there would have to be a reason for the limited number rather than an unlimited number. Yes, the both-and principle drives us on without end. Nor does the reality of an unlimited number exclude the reality of any finite number. The latter is just as real in itself as is the former. So then we can see why the number of realized possibles must be infinite, even as the series of arithmetical numbers must be infinite. Therefore we must declare: an infinite number of possible beings or kinds of being must timelessly be real.

But do you now ask: why should there be any possibles? What would give rise to them? Where would they come from? The answer is that they are implied in the apriori necessity we *had* to start with: there must be either being or no being. For this implied that there must be both being and non-being. But being itself implies possibles, since whatever is must be possible. We don't have to ask whence came these possibles. They are a self-evident necessity in themselves, since they are included in being. They have no source, no origin, they need none, they just have to *be*. No *mere* possibles!

Here is another way of stating the situation. We said, being implies possibles. Perhaps it would be better to say: being contains possibles. As noted, there are three basic notions, categories: being, nothing, possible. Now whatever has being has a *character*. That is why we have to think and speak about beings in propositions, with their subject typically a being, their predicate its character. "The rose is red." Where there is a character which could but doesn't exist, there is a *mere* possible. Such is the definition of possible: character just by itself. And whatever has being has existence *and* character. Thus being includes, contains, the possible. And nothing can exist without character. There is the definition of *nothing:* existence without character. Now we can see why *nothing* can have its own way of being, as it were; whatever has positive being has its character, *nothing* exists without any character—precisely the definition of nothing, non-being, as a present *fact*.

So when we say "there must be being and nothing" that means: all possible *kinds* of being, all possible *characters,* must exist. No *merely* possible characters are left, except of course in some limited created world such as ours which excludes a possible four, five or other dimensional space that might have been created.

Let us add a caution here—to be sure we said it above but it needs emphasis. You might think we are arguing thus: first of all there were endless possibles, as well as nothing at all. Then, by logical necessity, these possibles had to emerge into actual being. You might interpret the argument this way because we human beings are temporal and we naturally tend to think in terms of time. But of course what we have said has nothing to do with temporal sequence, with a *separate* realm of mere possibles which had to *become* real. Logical necessity is timeless! If *A* implies *B* by pure logic, *A* so far *is B*. The possibles must *be* real. We call them possibles because we are reasoning about what *can* be, and we discover that they *must* be.

Now look further and see what follows. The existence of any one possible implies the existence of any other, of all others. Inclusion is an apriori necessity. All are implicit in each, implicit as "folded in"—thereby they form *One* self-existent being. This Being is timeless, as logical necessity is timeless. Time is no apriori necessity. Perhaps you will say: time is a kind of being and so must be included in the One. But as we shall later stress, it is an exclusive way of being—it destroys the past and doesn't in the present moment include the possible future. The like also holds of space, with its particular dimensions. These kinds of being, such as they are *rather than* otherwise, need a causal explanation. No, only the possibles of utmost *simplicity* are united in the One, each one positive, just itself, too simple to contain any character which would exclude the presence of any other character.

And note this about the possible *goods* realized in this Being. Among such are outstanding to us humans the goods of power, intelligence, love. These must contain no exclusions, must be limitless. The same holds too of all other goods. The One must be *perfect*. Such is the One Infinite Being whom we name God. Here, notice, lies the justifying of this notion *perfection* which the Anselmian and other ontological arguments didn't account for. Instead of deriving God's being from His perfection as they would do, the present argument derives the perfection from the necessity of His existence as the fullest realization of all ultimate possibles, none conflicting. Thus our argument starts from scratch.

So we may say—to put it in terms of time so natural to our language—originally there was God, the Perfect One, and nothingness. And God the All-Knower knows the presence of nothingness outside Him, and as we shall see later, makes use of it in His Creation. But we would now stress this point: as chance is the realization of all possibles, all equally real, no preferences, no conflicts, our argument has shown that chance is an apriori timeless logical necessity, a wholly rational affair. Thus chance as properly understood shows the necessary being of God, the Perfect One, containing all values we can conceive—conscious mind, love, personality, and so on. True, you may say and some have said, God is too great to be a person, persons are limited beings. But as we have said, the greater doesn't exclude the less. God can be a person and be also much more.

One more point as to the Divine nature: it has the trait of polarity. We put this off for the moment, it will be more easily seen when we consider the relation of chance to love. Let us take up now some objections which might be made to the above—they will help us to see what is implied therein.

Some Implications

Start from the given fact of this world. It has its particular structure and behavior rather than some other possible structure and behavior—its three-dimensional space rather than four, five, or any other dimensions, its particular temporal laws such as gravitation, etc., rather than any others. So the principle of sufficient reason tells us that it must have a reason why, a cause. Wherefore we must say: God is its cause, its Creator—there is no other cause available. Remember what we said above, about the failure of determinism to find a cause! Yes, the principle of chance provides a cause, the First Cause of this actual world.

Look now at this matter of God's creative act. God is all possibles realized, no exclusions of one by another, *actus purus*, no mere possibilities in Him. Yet, being All-Powerful, He *can* create this particular world rather than some other which He *could* create.

Well, you object, doesn't this mean that there are in Him some *mere* possibles—the creation of any number of different worlds? And doesn't that imply that He is actually limited—He hasn't done all that He could do? No—there is no limitation here, just because there is present in Him the *power* to do all. The existence of this created world is one manifestation outside Himself, of that power. It is that outside world, something in *addition* to Him, which is the mere possible, made actual by His actual power. Do you say again: but then God

can't be infinite—He is limited, all reality is God plus the
world, it is greater than God. Of course that doesn't follow.
The infinite doesn't become finite if some finite things are
added to it, outside it. To be sure, we have assumed here that
God creates *freely,* whatever He creates. We shall later see
why He has freedom of choice. But even if what we have just
been arguing doesn't seem quite to answer the objection, we
may give another answer which doesn't limit the being and
power of God as the objection claimed. We might perfectly
well admit that there are possibles in God *in the sense that*
He may freely create as He wills. That is no limitation of His
actual being; in fact, it is an *addition* to His power of self-
existence.

Notice now by the way something of our world as implied
in the meaning of creation. Creation is causing to be: the
principle of sufficient reason applies to causing—why this
rather than that. So the created effect must be this rather than
that—in God's creating, this kind of a world rather than some
other. And that means *limitation,* some possible world outside
Him *selected*—a limitation of the principle of chance which
permits *all* possibles to be. So within any created world the
possibles are limited by *laws.* As we said above, a law is a
restriction of possible happenings, an exclusion, chance nar-
rowed down, limited. Yet chance, the original ultimate principle of being, essence of the Divine, could hardly be *wholly*
denied in the created world which, derived as it is from the
Divine, draws its positive traits from His nature, in however
limited a way. So there must be chance in a created world,
yet chance limited as that world is limited—hence there must
be *statistical* laws, not rigidly determined. Doesn't this then
show why rigid determinism in this world is not true?

Now for another point about Creation. Recall what we
said about the analogy of chance to the Democratic ideal. As
in that ideal each person is to be respected in and for himself,

so in God each kind of being, each trait is to be respected in and for itself. When He decides to create a group of these outside Himself, He does that, we may say, to reveal the value of its members as just by themselves in this selected group. He doesn't need to do that, He knows their values already; but He generously, freely, grants to these beings a realization of their values as it were in their group, their world, just by itself. That is why, as we are told in Genesis, Chapter I, what He had created was *very good*. Not perfect of course, being limited; but very good as containing the many values inherent in each part of the particular group and in all of them together. Perhaps the nearest analogy to this in our human life is when the artist makes a beautiful work, revealing the values in the selected objects just by themselves, his making done under no external compulsion, just because he enjoys doing it. And it is not so far from the play-motive, alike in the child and the adult. Maybe this is the truth in the claim of some recent Vedantists: Maya is not at all illusion, rather the joyous playful creation by the Divine Brahman. Of this play-motive more later: it deserves more respect than it has had for our theologians.

Return now to what we said about time and space not being included in God's nature: it needs emphasis, its implications are basic. Begin with the statement: all possibles realized in God imply one another, no possible can exclude, deny any other. "All things are possible in God." Now you object: "but not all things are *compossible* in God." For the possible systems of hypergeometry are not consistent with one another. Three-dimensional space excludes what higher-dimensional spaces may declare as axioms. Well, the answer, like all our argument so far, is extremely simply. To repeat what we said above: no one possible, being simply itself and no other, can deny, contradict any other. It is *not* any other, but *not* in the sense of otherness has of itself nothing to do with *not* in the sense of denial, exclusion of the being of another. The nature of each simple possible realized in God as just a positive character by itself, containing no reference to any others *except* the implication of those others existing, *cannot* just by itself deny any other. The reason why the hypergeometries, or any other kinds of world-system which we might conceive, conflict with one another is that the *axioms,* the laws on which each is based *do* to some extent at least deny those of other conceived systems. But the ultimate simple possibles we are here treating have no axioms, no laws in regard to the *characters* of other possibles, of one another; they are just their own positive characters. True, as we just said, they do imply the *being* of all the other possibles, as the doctrine of timeless chance asserts; but they do not imply anything *about* those others except their presence. There are no rigid *laws* governing them except the one rigid law of endless possibles, each realized by its own claim to be, its being also implied by the others and realized as just itself and no other. Yes, *in* God all things are possible, all are compossible. He is constrained by no laws except the one law that He must *be* as the fulfillment of all. There are no laws *in* God! It is only the laws we conceive when we think of all sorts of possible worlds other than God, laws which in any one world exclude other worlds, which give rise to the notion that *not* all possibles are compossible in God. It confuses God with the world.

Come now to the question: why *free* creation in God? Doesn't the principle of chance *compel* God to be precisely the perfect being He is, nothing more, nothing else permitted, still less implied? Isn't chance then just as compulsory as the rigid laws of the determinist? Doesn't it make God a static being? How can He originate His own activity, particularly a *free* activity doing this or that or whatever?

Free Creation

Chance respects each realized possible just for itself, making each exist for its own sake; its being and character not *caused* by any other. Each thereby has its individual value, its right to be; there is in it a certain note of independence, though not of any denial of another's right to be. Now in a created world, since it must be limited, this rather than that, there must be exclusions. But the very nature of chance dictates that there can be no apriori ground even in a limited world, for the exclusion of *this* particular rather than *that* particular. Whatever exclusion there is, whatever laws are present in a particular world, are under no compulsion to be what they are *except* by the act of the Creator. And there are no laws in God! So, mustn't His act of creation choose *freely* the kind of world He makes? Given His power to create, there is nothing to make Him create, say, a three-dimensional world rather than a four-dimensional one, and so for the other laws governing this or any other possible world.

But now you ask: whence this power to create? The above ontological proof tells us nothing about that, does it? It only tells us that God must be self-existent. It says nothing at all of possible *beings* outside, apart from God—in fact, it tells us that by logical necessity there is God and nothingness! True, this so far doesn't *forbid* something being *added* to this outside realm of nothingness. But what ground is offered to account for such an addition, due to the act of creation?

Come back to the principle of sufficient reason, the apriori complement, as we saw, of the principle of both-and, which brought to light the ontological proof. Reason itself sees that there is a possibility of *this* being real rather than *that,* provided there is a cause. Nor is this insight of reason drawn merely from observation of the events of our world. It is indeed suggested by such observation, but once suggested, it is seen by pure reason to be an apriori necessity. But further, it is implied in the meaning of chance. Chance is all-inclusive, yes, as seen in God's being. Yet, to repeat what we have just said, chance itself stresses the value of each realized possible just in itself. And as the good is the self-realization of the possible, the possibles realized in God being each in its own way good in itself—if they weren't they couldn't be combined into the perfection of God—they *could* be realized in a separate additional realm as existing quite by themselves if there is a cause at hand, a cause which the ontological proof has shown to be present. There is the special fruitfulness of the meaning of chance. It does *not* say, *only* the combination of all possibles is good; it says that each possible, each group of possibles, even if realized alone in conscious beings, could be a value, good. As the Thomist says, being itself is good. Again we see the note of independence. A created world may be a good world, must be such. The greater good, God, the Perfect One, cannot necessarily exclude the lesser good. Whence it is quite possible, consistent with the perfect good, to have the lesser goods *also*. It is the inclusiveness of chance which declares that the necessity of the Perfect Being implies the possibility that the less perfect elements and groups thereof may, owing to their own goodness *independent* of the goodness of others, show that independence by being made to exist apart, just by themselves. But this needs a cause, a reason why this rather than that, and the available cause is God! That is why God *can* create, has the power to create, yet without any compulsion to do so. His perfection is self-sufficient, it *needs* nothing more. Yes, creation is a free act, its *reason* for being present lies in the nature of chance. The old doctrine of creation as a *necessary* overflow of the Divine fullness has no ground.

Such then is the ontological proof and some of its implications. It remains for us to see that all this means the self-realization of love. As teaches the Christian doctrine of the Trinity, God as the Word, logos, reason, is one with God as love, the Holy Spirit. This now is where Agapology shows itself as the supremely *rational* metaphysic.

God As Love

So far we have in this chapter said little or nothing about love. We seem to have forgotten our title's new word Agapology. Why then did we seem to forget, to put off the question: why is God love? Because, as we said in Chapter I, the answer, core and center of our subject, is the *climax* of our argument. Love, God as love, we are to see, is the holy wedlock, the climactic union, of chance and reason. It is the living fact of their union, implied by and implying each and both together—the consummation of the both-and principle we stressed above.

But how can this be? As we asked in Chapter I, what has love, the warm-hearted moving urge in us living beings, to do with the cold abstractions we talked of so far—being, nothing, possible, chance? We said in Chapter III that there was available to us a way to the ontological proof, not by mere cold reason, but by the warm value-road, the "heart's reasons" in Pascal's terms. And we haven't been walking along that road at all! We have just immersed ourselves in the motionless timeless icy pool of abstract concepts. Well, we are now to see that, all unwitting, we *have* been treading the value-road, the *broadway* of love. We *have* been providing the logical justification of Pascal's words "the heart has its reasons". Yes, we are to see that God is self-existent *because* God is love, and God is love *because* He is self-existent.

Indeed, viewed in this light, the ontological argument may have an appeal which it wouldn't have from the cold impersonal viewpoint of reason alone. For it goes with the *fact* that in our hearts we do accept the supreme value of the love-motive—whatever justifies that value must be the truth. And recall what we saw in Chapter III: when some great good is experienced, directly felt, you do feel that it is self-justifying, no accounting for its existence needed. You just can't help feeling that way. Yes, our hearts do have a sense, a hint, of the ontological proof in their own way.

Begin then to seek the meaning of love, which has not been very much sought by our human philosophers.

What Is Love?

Here we repeat something we said in the book *Rational Religion*. When we truly love a person, we want that person to have the fullest, richest life possible. Don't confuse loving with liking, as is commonly done. To like is to want to be with, to enjoy the company of those we like, or sometimes even merely to approve, as when we like the President—which means we enjoy the thought of him and what he does. So love has often been understood as *merely* the urge to union with the beloved, sex-love the outstanding example. But the main motive in liking, though not necessarily the only motive, is *your own* pleasure. It is what has often been called the *Eros* motive, as distinct from *Agapé* which is our topic, the urge to the good of the loved one. True, it is easy usually, though by no means inevitable, to love those whom we like. One whom we like much we naturally want to keep, to preserve, for the joy his or her presence gives us, and the motive of preserving the goods of life for that person is lurking there. But it is not yet quite the motive of enriching that life, of helping that person to have the fullest possible development of all his or her capacities, potentialities for richest growth, *just for that person's own sake*. Of course this doesn't exclude liking, the joy *we* have in the presence of that loved one. Love knows no exclusions! Liking, which is so often a matter of self-love, is not against true love unless the self-love becomes exclusive, forgetting the needs of the other. True love, *Agapé,* knowing no exclusions, should *include* self-love *with* love of others. Jesus said: "Thou shalt love thy neighbor as thyself."

Now look further at the nature of love. We said, it means the realization of all possible potencies in the loved one. Nor is it limited to the love of human beings. We often love animals—which means preserving them, helping them to the fullest welfare permitted by their natures, and for their own sakes. So we would rule out all cruelty to animals—witness the S. P. C. A. We love our gardens; we would make them as fruitful and beautiful as can be, and for their own sakes too, as rich and good things in themselves. Love is always for individuals, be they lone ones or grouped together. If we love the group, the nation, class, race, the justification lies in loving the individuals therein and for their own sakes. And to realize the potencies in the loved one is to enrich, to make his life *better* and *better.* The realizing of potencies, none exclusive, is *good.*

Yes, love is the realizing of all possibles *without exclusion,* without conflict or frustration in the loved object. It is not a *mere* emotion, though it begins as one, and continues as one, emotion being the motive power within us. As motive it moves us to *act,* and so far as it doesn't do that it fails to be genuine love. True, it may fail to work out what it seeks, owing to some opposing power which is stronger, as when you urge a neighbor to help some good cause and for selfish reasons he refuses. But at least you must urge, so far as circumstances make it possible. Love includes action. And more, it includes knowledge. You must *know* what is good for the beloved, else your deed may prevent some good he should have. Also your deed, however helpful to him, shouldn't deprive someone else of his needed good. Love of one being, if genuine, cannot exclude love of any other being. Love is self-extending, self-increasing, once you really feel its beauty, which means once you really love. Of course, our native human loves are so exclusive! But the very fact that true love is love of the one for *his, her, its own sake,* implies that love should work for the good of each and of all. Each is himself, herself, itself, this individual with its needed goods—no reason whatever why one should have them more than another, so long as they don't conflict. "To each according to his needs!" Love has by its intrinsic nature a universal trend: it means that we should so minister to each that the conflicts will in the end disappear, which again means that we must survey the wide, wide world of all and *learn* what deeds work in that direction. That is what morality is: to discover the principles and methods which bring the greatest possible good to the greatest number, even to each and all in the end. Love is the moral law, which demands fullest intelligence and action.

See then the polarity here, the both-and principle. Jesus himself announced it when He said "thou shalt love thy neighbor as thyself." You should help one another, each for his own sake, *and* yourself also. Each is *both* to have his own goods realized and to realize the goods of others. See, too, how like chance in the ontological argument above this is: *all possible* goods should be realized, and at the same time the goods of each one are good *just by themselves*—a note of independence and *with it* the necessary connection of all these goods, each helping the others *as well as himself.* But more of this point in a moment.

Still you may say, love differs from chance in this: love is the realizing of all possible *goods* in the object, chance is the same with respect to all *facts,* good or not good. To be sure— we repeat—our English language says "Give every one his chance", and we defend the ideal of equal *opportunity* for all. But that means opportunity for getting his needed *goods.* Mere realization of possibles, it seems, has of itself nothing to do with good. When you toss your coins and all the possible

combinations are realized in the long run, there isn't anything
good about it. And so with the statistical laws of the non-
living world; where is there anything good in their being
statistical rather than rigid? In fact, there seems to be something rather denying than implying any goodness there. Whatever is good in these laws surely lies in their regularity, in their
orderly character rather than in the minute variations. It is
their order which enables us to foresee the future and adapt
our conduct to that future. And further, order is admirable,
beautiful, we love to see it, we love it as a good thing in itself,
and we want to see it preserved. We abominate a disorderly
situation. Isn't that why so many scientists in the past have
believed in a rigid determinism? They *loved* its perfect order,
every law exactly fulfilled, no deviations allowed. As we have
said, it gratifies the needs of intellect, everything explained.
And the religious ones have used this as an argument for
God's being: the argument from design as seen in nature's law
and order to an intelligent designer of all, First Cause. Yes,
there is something divine about order! Even the scientist with
his alleged detachment from emotion, loves the beautiful order
in the universe, and strives to discover more and more of it in
the remotest nebulae and the finest ultra-microscopic wavicles.
Well then, doesn't the chance-element mean chaos so far? To
be sure, these little variations are so small that they don't spoil
the order on the grand scale, the order of the heavens, even
the order of man's environment in his tiny planet. Isn't it a
good thing that they are so very small? No, surely on the face
of it, chance doesn't seem to have much to do with goodness.
How could it be akin to love the supreme good? But now look
a little deeper.

How Chance And Love Are One

After all, there is a beauty all its own in chance, in spite
of its seeming denial of order. It contributes in its own way

to order. It has the note of symmetry, of balance. The variations in statistical law *even up* in the course of events realizing the law. Chance restores what at first it seems to take away. If at one moment the variations are greater in one direction, that is counterbalanced later. Yet it does, as it were, give a *degree* of freedom to each event, respecting, so to speak, the individuality of that event, allowing it to act in its own individual way, to however small a degree. And it does this to all the events within the law equally, no preference in the long run. Isn't there here at least an analogy to the love-motive? According to the determinist, as we said above, the individual event has no right of its own to show its individuality, it is wholly compelled, enslaved by the law, no respect for it as *itself*. Individuality vanishes. But chance as now understood respects the individual. Yes, it *combines* respect for the beauty of order with respect for the rights of the individual to be itself and no other. So much for chance in the inorganic realm. Of course all this is so far but an *analogy* to the love-motive which is centered on the good. There is no *actual* good in the inorganic *merely* by itself, apart from the conscious mind which *appreciates* it, brings to light its otherwise unrealized good.

Recall now what we saw in Chapter II about life's evolution with its innumerable chance-mutations. Surely it is very good that in spite of the evils of many destructive ones and the conflicts emerging between the species and between the individuals as they evolved, the process gave rise to the wide and widening arena of human goods. Yes, there is *something* of the good in chance. Remember, too, that this evolution was due to the occurrence of uncountable mutations, as if to realize the maximum possible number. True again, this is but an analogy in the unconscious realm of mutations to what love is in the conscious: to realize all possible goods in the beloved. But now see what chance is when it holds, as we saw above, of the ultimate possibles all realized in one self-existent Being.

Come back to what we said of God's oneness. As chance means the actual being of *all* these possibles, the being of any one of them implies the being of every other. That is the law of timeless chance: if one is real, all must be real *equally,* no preference of this rather than that. The oneness is this mutual implication. If *A* implies *B* timelessly, *A* contain*s B,* is *B.* Implication is the oneness of the different! In our world of temporal laws *A* the present event contain*s B potentially* as an event to come. In the timeless realm of being, if *A* implies *B, A* actually is one with *B.* And if *B* implies *A, B* also is one with *A.* So as the reality of each possible implies the reality of all others, each contains, is, all together, all fused into an absolute inseparable unity, the self-existent One. Difference doesn't exclude sameness, each may include the others. What then does this union of sameness and difference mean?

It means that God must be a conscious mind, nothing of the unconscious in Him. Here we come to a fundamental point, so far as we know not yet specifically emphasized by any thinker. What is it, to be conscious? It is to have an object other than yourself present in yourself. In our world of space with its exclusions, its separation of beings, this cannot *wholly* be the case, only partly so. The tree you are conscious of isn't as an actual tree completely in your mind. It is in your mind as *what* it is, not in its actual existence. It exists whether or not you are aware of it. And your practical mind knows that whatever the Berkeleyan idealist may assert, the tree exists outside your mind. Material objects, separate and mutually exclusive as they are, cannot *so far* be part of a conscious mind. So in the realm of ultimate possibles realized there can be no material things, because that realm, with all its differences between the possibles, is yet absolutely one. To each element in it all the others are immediately present, present as and in themselves actual. In short, consciousness is the very essence of God. It is not merely one among an endless collection of traits, one which is bound to be realized side by side with all the others. It is that, but it is infinitely more, since it is the very principle of union between all. So we can see why God *must* be pure consciousness, or as we say, spirit.

And with conscious mind or spirit the good can be present, as it couldn't be without that. How then does it come in?

Each element, so to call it, implies all the others, respects, demands, their being. Not only does it so far include their being, it also respects their being as just themselves. Chance respects each particular for itself. As each implies all the others, each is fulfilling the possibility of the others in implying their realization, their being. In God, the purely conscious Being, each element is contributing thereby to the being of all the others, the being which is the fulfilling of their potentiality to exist. And this is God's conscious life: He *feels* everything within Him helping everything else within Him to be. It is all positive, no frustrations, conflicts, exclusions. And that is what good means: the fulfillment of potentialities, possibles resident in the nature of the conscious being. If you ask why fulfillment is good, the answer lies in your direct experience. Always you *feel* that the fulfillment of your desire is good. You can't help it. If that fulfillment frustrates some other, so far its good is diminished. But as in the Divine nature there are no conflicts, no frustrations, there is as we have seen, all possible good, *perfection.* Do you object that there is no desire in God, whereas good is always the fulfillment of desire? True, desire is with us a temporal affair and God is timeless. But the logical necessity of the fulfillment of all possibles in God is the *timeless* form of desire fulfilled. Indeed as we have declared in *Rational Religion* (p. 32), even in our common experience of happiness there is a timeless phase—happiness as desire fulfilled, no change desired. In happiness we want what we have got.

Now as the last step in the argument, hardly a step indeed, rather a tautology in view of what we just said, we come to the climax, the feature which makes the argument an Agapology. Obvious it is that the good which has just revealed itself is love, just straight pure love. It fits the definition of love perfectly: conscious realization of all the potencies of the object with no frustrations. So every element in God the conscious One loves every other element. God, the One including all, thereby loves all the elements. And as our argument above stated stems from chance we can but conclude: timeless chance in God is love. God is love, pure and perfect. We are commanded to love God first of all. Yes, to love God is to love love, which is to love all possible good for all beings. Hence the necessity of the second commandment: brotherly love. Love is the fulfilling of the law, its logical necessity.

So the answer to the mystery of being implies the *fact* of value, of love, which can exist in conscious mind only. God's being is the self-realization of the good, of love. Now we can see *why* the good is with us self-realizing. It is self-realizing in us His creatures because He made us able to experience that trait, goodness, which is a self-realizing one—perfect in Him, however limited in us.

So this meets the objection above made, that chance is cold, impersonal, unconscious, utterly remote from warm personal love. It is chance that timelessly produced the conscious good, the perfect conscious good which is God. And the way of producing is the way of love, realizing all possibles in Him as spirit, those realized possibles in Him being *goods* as they are the *fulfillment* of all possibles, timeless trends to which our human temporal desires are analogous, such fulfillment being the essence of good, of the supreme good which is love.

Note also that we have answered the objection which said:

goodness can't be realized unless there is already some being or beings in whom it can be realized. We have seen that chance—the realization of all possibles—itself brings about the *Being* in Whom the good must be realized. And, as this chance is an apriori logical necessity, God as love is the unity of chance and reason.

Now recall what we said in Chapter I about our title and its relation to the philosophy of Charles S. Peirce, as brought out in the collection of his papers by Morris Cohen entitled *Chance, Love, and Logic*. We here claim to have done what Peirce didn't try to do, to show that these three are truly one. And there is in this oneness, as we suggested above, a note which may well recommend the ontological proof to those who would naturally feel bound to resent it. God is self-existent because God is love. When we view God as love, love His complete essence identical with His existence, we can see His existence in a light which no other angle of view can give, a light which warms our hearts and beckons our reason. Yes, we have really been using the Franciscan approach, the way opened by Pascal when he said "the heart has its reasons". All because chance, in its modern and proper sense, *is* ultimately the same principle as love. Alas that the philosophers and theologians haven't yet approached the mystery of God's being through the door of either love or chance!

Let us now by the way call attention to another alleged mystery, accepted as such by most Christians, even denied as illogical by some. (We here repeat what we said in *Rational Religion*, Chapter III, with some needed additions.) This is the dogma of the Blessed Trinity: God is three, God is one, God is three in one. Note the word *dogma*. It means that this has been revealed to us by God Himself in the teaching of the Son and His Church and therefore must be accepted though we cannot understand why it is so. Yet the devout Thomist, prizing reason as he does, believes that it is in itself

wholly rational, logically implied in the very being of God,
though far, far above our ability to see why. But our claim
here is that as we *can* understand clearly God's self-existence,
so we can understand what the Trinitarian Christians have
taken, it would seem, as the mystery next to God's self-
existence in its distance above our comprehension. This *doctrine*—we don't see it as dogma—is a logical necessity following from what we have above seen, a wholly intelligible truth.

For it goes with the three principles: chance, logic, love.
Chance, which is God's self-existence, designates God as
power: He makes Himself exist. His power to create a world
follows from this: if He can make Himself exist, certainly He
can make lesser beings, limited worlds, exist. So does Christianity the love-religion, speaking in terms of the natural human
example, family love, call Him the Father, the First Person.
To be sure, we here interpolate, we have elsewhere said that
God might qually well be called *Mother*—some sects have so
done—perhaps even a little more fittingly, as in our human
analogy mother-love is usually stronger than father-love. But
in past history the male has been the outstanding public figure,
the one showing power in big public deeds—hence the title
Father has been the natural one, giving the note of creative
power. Logic, reason, the Word, is God the Second Person,
the Divine *nature* revealed in the *truths* and *principles* taught
in the words and deeds of Christ—again in family terms the
Son, earthly embodiment of the Father in the flesh. And of
course love is the Holy Spirit, Third Person. At the same time
the identity of the three—chance, logic and love being one
and the same as well—means the Oneness of God. The three
Persons are not *separate* individuals.

We said above that we would come to see that polarity is
a necessary character of God when we realized that love, the
essence of God, is one with reason and chance. So now we
can do that. It is brought to light in the doctrine of the

Trinity. As we have said, the First Person implies the Second Person, and the Second implies the First. And this mutual implication, uniting them so as to give perfection in power and reason, *both,* realized in the Divine unity, is love—love the perfect realization of all ultimate possibles, the perfect good. It is the principle of *both-and,* which solved for us the mystery of being. Each of the two Persons, perfect power and perfect intelligence, is good in itself, at the same time each by the principle of love implies, leads to the fact of the other. *Both* signifies the union by love, *and* signifies the being and value of each in itself. There is the polar union.

In the next chapter we shall see that this principle of the Divine Trinity is the source of a principle verified in our human history, indeed elsewhere too: a principle which will guide us when we consider, as we shall there do, the problem of evil. It is in our *temporal* world what we have in Chapter I called the *Law of the Three Stages:* power the first stage in human progress, intellect the second, love the third and the climax. Indeed this law is fundamental in life: it holds of evolution as a whole, of mankind's progress through the ages, even of the life today of the human individual.

But of course all this argument of ours does *not* mean that *all* truth about God and His creation can be discovered by our intellects, limited as they are. Intellect needs help! No doubt man couldn't get what he so far has without *some* revelation. St. Thomas too taught that. God the Supreme Lover knowing man's weakness, gave him supernatural truths which he would not have discovered merely by reasoning from the facts of this world. Our argument accepts this. But it adds its own complement: these revelations are given not only as a moving power guiding our conduct but also as a motive power to our intellect. Our loving Creator loves to promote our understanding more and more. His revelations are a *stimulus* to our intelligence. No exclusions! Our religion hasn't yet overcome the native human trend to put some one agent quite above the rest—in this case the grace of God completely, absolutely above our possible understanding. After all, as He gives us health and strength to act as He would have us act, advancing more and more, however slowly, through the long course of evolution in the love-life, surely He would give us the ability to understand more and more of His revelation as our intelligence grows in that long course. God's grace isn't *only* something we must passively accept, it is a loving urge from Him to act better by our own wills, to think better by our intellects. It is the thesis of the present book that if we are willing to look we can know much more about our Perfect Creator than is admitted even by the theologians.

So much for the ontological proof through the road of love—which is also the road of reason. Now we ought to meet some at least of the many objections which are sure to be raised, even by devout Christians. Of these we select but one—what seems to be the gravest of all—the presence of evil in God's created world. How could the Perfect One create a world in which there has been through the long ages a vast amount of evil, and still is today? Surely this contradicts the Agapologist's claim that God is love. Well, we shall see that the answer to this most troubling objection, impossible as it looks, comes forth from just that which it seems to deny, that God is the Perfect Lover. But its difficulty makes it demand a chapter by itself.

CHAPTER V

THE PROBLEM OF EVIL

This problem confronts us, first of all, because from the apriori necessities above seen there seems to be no possible way of explaining how the Divine nature *could* permit the presence of evil in His created world. The effect draws its nature from the cause—from what other source could it do so? In God, the Perfect Being, there is not even the slightest hint of the possibility of evil—how could it be found in His creatures? Could it perhaps be because the created world must be limited? No, there is no logical implication in the notion of limitation which makes evil a necessity. Evil, which as we have seen is frustration, is much more than limitation. Good and evil are possible only to conscious minds. And even if the goods of those minds are limited, that doesn't imply that they are frustrated. Why not a world in which every such mind can and does attain all the limited goods it wants? Indeed, if creation of a limited world implied the necessity of evil therein, God in creating it would be *compelled* to create evil, a fact contradicting His perfection. Or perhaps, while a limited world doesn't imply the necessity of evil, it might imply the possibility of evil. But this only means that if He created at all He would be *compelled* to admit the possibility of something quite foreign to His nature—and whence could that possibility be derived? Surely there is nothing whatever in His nature that makes evil even a possibility in His creation, perfect as He is. Or put it this way: it would seem that the only way of introducing evil therein would be to have the goods of the various minds conflict, or at least to make it possible that they might conflict. How then could the creation by the Perfect One in whom no goods can possibly conflict give rise even to the possibility of what is wholly against His nature?

No, the problem isn't only to see *why* God permits evil; it is first of all to see how He *could* permit it. Even His supreme power, it would seem, couldn't let Him create a world containing what contradicts His nature as the cause of that world. So far as the present writer knows, this primary problem has scarcely been treated at all. Come to it then!

How Evil Could Come Into God's Creation

Recall what we said above, putting it as we did in temporal language: originally there was God and nothingness, *nothing* as we called it. This nothing was wholly other than God, outside Him. Now recall also the statement so often made: God created the world *ex nihilo*, from out of nothing. *Nothing* was there, so to say, all the time, and God the all-knower was aware of it, knew that it would always be present *with* His creation, ready at hand for Him to *use* it in that creation, for some *good* purpose. As we saw in Chapter IV, *nothing* is everywhere and always present in our world. He *has* used it in His creating. Well, this presence of *nothing* will enable us to see how evil in the creatures, evil which cannot come from God, may come to be in them as contributed by the factor of nothing, itself quite outside Him, yet *used* by Him.

How then could this factor *nothing,* extreme negation as it is, give rise to the possibility at least, if not the necessity, of evil? Now look at a certain character of this world, wherein conscious minds are *embodied*.

A Trait Of Physical Being

Conscious minds in our created temporal world occupy separated bodies. A body in one place cannot be a body in another place at the same time. The motion of one body cannot be the motion of another body. And with this separation, we shall see, evil can arise. How then could God make this separation? There is none of it in Him. Here is where He has used the fact of nothingness, outside Him. To be this body separated from that body is to have each contain *nothing* of the other, nothing indeed of *any* other. That alone can explain how God *could* endow the creatures with a trait which did not come from Him: negation which is not present in Him. Recall again the assertion we made above: the actual presence of nothing everywhere and always. This body is here in just this place and *nothing* in addition to it is here in just this place. The otherness which is in Him goes with sameness, no exclusion, becomes in the realm outside Him where *nothing* is present, where He creates positive beings each with nothing else also present with it—becomes an otherness which excludes, denies sameness, makes separation.

See now how in this world with conscious minds in separate bodies could evil enter. Such a world would naturally have its *laws,* limited as it must be—laws as we saw in Chapter I are limitations of possible events. Well, the laws constraining the movements of each body, *could* doubtless on occasion make this and that body clash. Somewhere, it seems, there would be, perhaps even must be such events. And we do see them, due to our law of gravitation, as when a heavy body falls to earth and smashes another body which it hits—often itself too. Opposing forces would naturally be generated in a universe where bodies and their movements exclude one another. And when living bodies come on the scene, some physical forces there would be which now and then lead to their injury, even demolish them. But when conscious minds dawn in these living bodies, such events are felt as bad, evil. Yes, it is the separateness due to the presence of *nothing* throughout the world which makes possible *some* evil at least, evil not at all due to the Divine nature but to the *nothing* which He introduced into the world. And note by the way that this which enables us to explain how God *could* permit evil, *as He has done,* confirms what we claimed about the presence of nothing in the world.

But we may go further in this confirmation. For the above evils are by no means the only ones due to the exclusions, the separations. There is one greater evil, seemingly inevitable too. Each human being, each conscious animal, is located in one particular body *and no other,* after it is born into the world. Each so far as it is conscious wants to continue its own bodily life and the goods it contains first and foremost; being a separate body it does not so far want to do the like for another living conscious body. Many exceptions of course have entered the scene in the course of evolution—that we shall later dwell on. But deepest of all native exclusive trends in conscious life is this one, due to the fact of separate bodies, that each has an inborn urge to seek its own goods, indifferent to the goods of others, and when they conflict with its own, as may well sometimes happen, to exclude them, frustrate them. If we could live in their bodies we should want their goods, but we don't and can't—except for two outstanding instances to be immediately noted which actually confirm what we have just said. Yes, when you and I want the same thing—the same piece of food, the same jewel, even the same woman!— as will sometimes happen, there enters conflict, fighting, frustration of life's goods for one of us at least. All due to the physical separation of the spatial bodies in which dwell the conscious minds!

This Explanation Confirmed

As we just said, this is confirmed when we look at two examples of separation disappearing, two of the commonest human experiences, sex-love and parentage. Here separation's disappearance naturally goes with the good increasing. In sex-love the lovers long for *bodily* union. Part of the man enters the body of the woman; to that degree their bodies fuse in joyous unity. A purely animal instinct, you say, mere physical lust. So it often is, perhaps too often. Yet the bodily union may be and for many lovers has been, is, and will be a matter of tenderest love, each sensing and promoting the joyous feelings of the other, loving the other self as one's own self. And note, the resulting *union* of sperm with ovum gives rise to a new human being, a creative gain. Still more, and with fewer exceptions, is the like confirmed in parentage, especially in mother-love. The mother contains the child, the child is wholly within her, part of her, nourished as her body is nourished. Isn't that why mother-love is normally, typically, the most intense and enduring of human loves? It begins by overcoming *completely* the exclusion due to space, and is normally continued too for a time by the external contact of feeding the baby at the breast. These two are the supreme human instances. Indeed the same character to some degree is seen even the natural longing to touch the loved being, to fondle, caress. But alas! these experiences are limited to parents, lovers, even friends; they hardly go further with most of us. If only we could overcome *wholly* the bad influence of the separation of our bodies!

Well, doesn't this answer the first problem about evil: how *could* the Perfect One make a world with evil in it? But now comes the graver question: why *would* He do that? Doesn't it contradict what we saw in Chapter IV; God is perfect love? Why *would* the Perfect Lover create a world with so much suffering in it? Wouldn't it be cruel in Him to do so? And as to wickedness, sin, moral evil, which no doubt *deserves* punishment, suffering in the wicked one, wouldn't it be cruel in Him to permit what deserves suffering?

Why Evil Did Come In

Yes, we come now to the problem of evil as usually treated by past and present thinkers. It is generally put thus: if God the perfectly *good* being creates a world with evil, that shows that He can't be all-powerful, as is claimed. He may do the best He can, but He isn't powerful enough to prevent some evil at least. And, on the other hand, if He is all-powerful, omnipotent, and makes such a world as this, He can't be perfect in love. He cannot be *both* omnipotent and perfectly good if He creates a world with evil in it. Yet our argument above has claimed that He *is* both, even as has the devout Christian through the centuries. How can we possibly escape this conclusion: He let evil exist because He had to!

Well, let us state the answer we shall give, however strange, however easily refuted it looks to be at first: the above statements overlook the *temporal* character of this world, the all-important fact of *time*. As we shall argue, and by empirical evidence too, there is every reason to declare that God made such a world with its evils so that His creatures would *sooner or later* have far more and greater good than they *could* have had without the presence of evils. Didn't Jesus say: "there is greater joy in heaven over one sinner that repenteth than over ninety and nine just ones who need no repentance"? What we shall say is quite in line with this. We shall see that there is in our world's basic constitution a *trend,* many trends, to overcome the separateness which is the source of so much evil—nay more, there is something in the very nature of evil which tends to its own destruction—destruction by a greater good than there could have been without the evil, a good realized by the work of conscious minds, making them stronger, better, greater than they could otherwise be. Now look first at some trends in the make-up of this world which at least point toward the vanishing of evil, toward a *time* when it has gone into the unreal past, when there is no longer the fact of evil, no problem of evil.

Nature's Trend To Union Of The Separate

One such trend is obvious in the evolution of life, proceeding as it has done from the simplest to more complex unity in the living bodies. The more differentiated and distinct the parts in the higher organisms, the more has their unity overcome the spatial exclusion of the parts. The unity of a tree, a man, has overcome more of the spatial separation than the unity of a moss, insect, amoeba. And in mankind there is a degree of unity extending beyond the individual body. Sex-union joins separate individuals into the family, living *together*. And further, mankind groups itself into the clan, tribe, nation—all this a trend to union in one way or another. Man is a social being. And today we have bridged over our separation more and more, as with the telephone, radio, speeding plane, and such.

Yes, even in the non-living realm there has been a like trend. Our scientists have of late revealed a very, very slow change through billions of years in material being, a change toward union of the separate. Read the fascinating account in the book *From Galaxies to Man* by John Pfeiffer (New York, Random House, 1959). As far back as we can trace, our universe was a vast fog, scattered in every direction; the steady trend since then has been toward consolidation. "Slowly matter drifted together in a kind of inanimate herd instinct . . . matter stirred and thickened" (p. 5). Definite bodies were slowly formed, separate bodies indeed, yet each a fairly solid unity—from atoms, molecules, up to planets and stars. What is solidity but the sticking together of the parts? Then organization came on, the structured law-abiding atom, molecule, solar system, nebula, the *system* of each from atom to galaxy. Organization means that the elements of a body or group are separate in space yet are not independent of one another, each contributing to the position and motion of the rest. We might say, the history of the great universe has been the trend toward overcoming the *mere* separateness due to its space. Extensions bunched themselves into unities, organized, parts contributing to one another.

And this "holistic" trend, as the philosophers call it, has, as we said, permeated the living body even when there is no consciousness, as in the plants. Yes, there is on the whole throughout nature, living and non-living, a trend to the overcoming of mere separateness, and most of all in the living *organisms*. Think again for the latest example which has come about today, of the "one world" brought forth in our human life by the telephone, radio, plane, and such. With all its increased conflicts, mankind is a closer knit group than ever before. Distance has lost much of its power. There may be more fighting at present, as conflicting interests of different nations come closer together; yet at the same time our wars, hot and cold, are stirring up a greater and greater urge for a harmonious world.

Come now to a further point: the very nature of evil makes possible, if not inevitable, a trend within it to vanish, to be replaced by the trend to unity—a unity which yields the presence of love.

Evil's Natural Trend To Vanish

Here, as with the ontological argument above, note the simplicity of the reason for this trend. Frightfully complicated as are the evils in our human life, their nature and consequent trend to be abolished are revealed by the utterly simple definition of evil which we shall bring to light.

Evil comes only with conscious mind, and conscious minds live in separate bodies in our world. It would seem—and many religious ones have declared—that the principal source

of evil for us lies in the exclusive body, the "wicked flesh".
Not that this is the whole truth; we shall later stress the goodness of the body too. But now look at this factor *mind,* without which there could be no evil, and see something in its
nature which makes this evil tend to vanish. Given conscious
mind, we affirm, evil reveals evil's trend to disappear. If the
mind's body makes evil real, the body's mind brings out the
inherent trend of evil to destroy itself. Not, of course, that this
trend in the conscious body applies to all kinds of evil. Other
factors are needed to provide a trend for evils which are not
just of the body. But the bodily evils are many and deep and
it is important to note *their* trend to disappear.

See then something in the long course of our history on
earth and in the flesh. We have learned, and more rapidly
of late, how to make the body more capable of getting what
it wants—increasing health, strength, length of life, overcoming much sickness, almost abolishing many diseases. Such has
been the great progress of medicine—a social not a self-
centered good. Mankind has worked slowly and increasingly
toward the ideal marriage of mind and body—*mens sana in
corpore sano.* And why this overall trend? Just because to our
conscious minds the *pains* of bodily weakness, sickness, death,
are *felt* as evils and we would abolish them. It was pain, suffering, that urged its own disappearance.

Nor is this trend of pain to be removed confined to the
realm of the body. There is in our mental, spirit-life a motive
for goods such as affection, fair dealing, peace of mind, doing
the work we love. Whatever is felt as frustrating these is taken
as evil, disagreeable, painful to a degree, and we would remove it. It is the *unpleasant* quality, the painfulness, that
urges us to do so. Yes, evil in the last analysis is pain, suffering,
unhappiness of whatever sort. And recall the definition of
pain: it is that which by its very nature urges its own removal

while we have it. See then why evil has in it a trend toward vanishing.

An Objection Met

But of course many of our good moralists would deny that evil is essentially pain. They would say that this or that deed is evil in itself, quite independent of its leading to some painful result. It is *wrong* to lie, to steal, and so on, no matter what the consequence. And we *know* it is wrong, just as we know brotherly love is good in itself. It is our moral sense that tells us this. Or if you don't admit a native moral sense, you will say the deed is wrong because God has forbidden it. And there is in these views of the right and wrong no *inherent* trend in evil to be abolished. They take the right, the morally good, as a *command,* whether given by the moral sense or by the Almighty God. It would, they declare, degrade the moral law to connect it with the petty emotions of pain and pleasure. Well, the best evidence that they are mistaken is seen in their religion, if they have one. They assert that if you do wrong you will be tormented in hell, and if you do right you will enjoy eternal bliss in heaven. They can't get away from the pain-pleasure motive. A mere command to do no wrong has just by itself no urge sufficient to abolish the free choice of the sinner to disobey if he wants to. And if he can go on disobeying time after time, no *penalties* resulting, there is no solution of the problem of evil, since evil may continue with no tendency to its removal. No reason why God the Perfect Lover would have permitted evil to enter! Yes, commands need reinforcing, they are obeyed from fear or from respect for the commander—and such respect means a *satisfaction* in carrying out his orders. As a fact the course of human progress through the ages verifies this. Mankind has advanced, as we noted above, by learning to reduce its pains and to increase peaceful cooperation for gaining the goods of life, and as to his moral gains, due to his religion, the fear of hell has been a powerful agent.

To be sure this native trend of evil to disappear is no straight compulsion. It is but a help, making the choice to concentrate your efforts on the good grow easier, however slowly. We might say: God has seen to it that the choice of the good is not too difficult for us. He eases it for us gradually as our history goes on, though of course not enough to dismiss our responsible choice.

Well, this so far does look toward confirming the answer we announced to the question: why did God permit evil? If it is inherent in the very nature of evil to *stimulate* us to remove it by our own active effort, thereby making ourselves stronger and better, surely that does suggest, if not necessarily imply, that someday in the future, however far away, we shall abolish it wholly. After all, didn't He give us *time* to do this? Isn't that why He created a temporal world?

Time Offering A Solution?

Let us here note, as tending toward confirming this suggestion, how the views of the nature of time have changed in mankind's philosophies. There is a striking contrast between the older views and those of many today. As an example of the former, recall the teaching of Gautama: time is but the succession of events which repeat the same general situation over and over again. The Wheel of Existence rolls on endlessly, repeating its evil frustrations, no escape from evil in this world of time. The only escape from evil is found in the experience of the timeless Nirvana. The capital N in this word denotes the negation, the abolishing of all desire, desire the temporal source of evil in our lives. See then the contrast between such a view and the modern view of time as a *value,* a principle working for the goods of this world. Only in the later centuries, and especially now, after the fact of evolution was discovered, has come up this notion of time as the principle of progress to the better and better in this world. It is indeed a great landmark in the history of man's thinking. See how it has penetrated the minds of our later philosophers! Think of the systems produced by Bergson, Alexander, Whitehead, Dewey, Hartshorne, Lloyd Morgan, and, among the Thomists today, Teilhard de Chardin. We call these systems *Process Philosophies*—a distinctly modern new departure. Of course the emphasis on change, on time as a basic fact, is old, as in the Greek philosophers—e.g., Heraclitus—but it is now made central as the keynote to the *good,* the principle of progress, increasing good, decreasing evil. Like the rolling snowball—Bergson's example—for these thinkers time as it rolls on increases the volume of good by preserving the old and adding more and more new goods. To repeat what we said above, it is what Arthur Lovejoy named the principle of plenitude—see his account of its gradual dawning on the minds of the philosophers in his masterly work *The Great Chain of Being.* That principle is indeed the temporal form of what we have defended above, the principle of chance, the gradual realization of all positive possibles. And these process-philosophers, using the evidence of historical fact, have taken it more or less to be a fundamental law of reality—though they don't call it chance. Yet if our proposed ontological proof above is right, mustn't this chance-principle, plenitude, apply to God's creation, whose positive principles are derived from His nature?

But of course here appears what is perhaps the most troubling of all objections: what of our free choice? Won't it *always* be possible for some conscious beings to choose their own exclusive goods and frustrate the goods of others? Let us then consider a suggestion which admits this and yet might seem to offer an answer.

A Practical Solution?

We start with the claim to have proved the necessary existence of the Perfect Lover. And as He has created a world with evil in it, this seems to contradict His perfect love. So we proposed, to remove the contradiction, that if He permits the entrance of evil, that *must* be because it can bring about a greater good than would be possible without it. What is that greater good? It is the growing realization in His children that evil *can* be destroyed *if they so will*. He gave us free choice that we might by *our own effort* abolish our evils. If everything went right always with us, if we always did right with no effort *of our own* we would be mechanical robots. God the perfect lover, valuing us for our own sakes, would give us the opportunity to become good in ourselves by overcoming evils by our own individual work. See then: the solution of the problem of evil is no theoretical matter, no matter of *reasoning* about the future. It turns on our individual free choices. It might be the case that there will always be some who choose to do wrong, to frustrate the love-motive. On the other hand, it might be that all conscious beings would come to fulfill this motive and evil would wholly vanish. The solution of the problem of evil has been *entrusted to us!* No, there is no logical necessity which of itself dictates the final vanishing of all evil in the created world. The solution is a *practical* business. There is no logical demonstration that either of the alternatives above will be the final fact. It is all up to *us* to solve the problem!

A Rational Solution Needed

Yet even if we admit this practical answer, there comes again the old objection. Suppose we don't, all of us, carry out this practical solution. Then the problem of evil isn't solved. God the Perfect One, loving all creatures, lets some of them continue their evils, perhaps through all the future. How could the Perfect Lover have these evils continue on and on? Or perhaps He would destroy the sinners if they never repent? Would a true lover cause the destruction of those he loves if he has the power to save them—a power which God the all-powerful certainly has? Yes, even if justice—a good in itself—requires their eternal torment in hell, so far evil does continue; what greater evil could there be than eternal torment?

The Law Of The Three Stages

Well, there is now at hand some empirical evidence that eventually the evils of the created world will be destroyed. If we look at the course of evolution in conscious life—for such life only can there be evil—we find a certain *law* pervading it, a law which, if we examine its implications, does look well-nigh to guarantee the disappearance of evil sooner or later, no matter if we do have free choice. Recall what we noticed toward the end of Chapter I and again at the end of Chapter IV, where we spoke of the *Law of the Three Stages* in mankind's history. We are now to verify its presence and power. And—to repeat—the most notable thing in this law is, we shall see, its temporal analogy to the Divine Trinity, Whose nature as Cause of the world *must* be expressed in this temporal law, since the effect draws its nature from the cause. Surely now a *law* empirically verified is the best assurance of what should be expected for the future of conscious minds. And so far as the present writer knows, notice of this law has never been taken in all the discussion of the problem of evil. Come then to the witness thereof in this temporal arena, witness in different realms therein too.

Three Stages In Biological Evolution

We repeat from Chapter I, look at the course of evolution in animal life. There was a long period in which each animal was concerned to continue its life by its own bodily activity, its ability to react against hostile forces. The more of its power to do that, the more likely it was to survive. It scarcely reflected about what to do; its successful reactions were due to the lucky mutations which occurred, giving it the *power* to behave thus and so. Even when mankind with its dawning intelligence came on the scene, that trait was used to prolong its owner's life in the main by gaining more *power* against destructive forces of nature and of animal and human enemies. This was the first stage in the evolution of conscious minds, the power-motive. The strongest survived.

Then came the greater development of intelligence in mankind, knowledge about the ways of nature and of the living beings around him, knowledge enabling him to foresee what was likely to happen and to adjust his behavior thereto in new ways that wouldn't occur to the lower forms which survived just by their strength. This increasing success due to intelligence, thought, reflection, gave it a value to its owner, a growing respect for intelligence, and it gradually came to be considered a good in itself, in its own right, to be cultivated more and more.

And with this growth in intelligence, knowing more and more about the ways to preserve and increase life with its goods, it was inevitable that man would come to see: *first,* how cooperation with his fellows could prolong his own life and its goods, then *later* as this cooperation continued and increased, that his fellows, like himself, have *their* goods, which they need and want as much as he needs and wants his own —and so their goods should be promoted too. Even if as yet he had no purely altruistic motive in his inheritance and mutations, his increasing intelligence would tend toward that motive. Knowledge, a good in its own right with its felt urge to increase, *must* as it comes to know more about human nature, bring to light a good which hadn't yet been felt, a respect for the needs of others for their own sake, the dawning of the love-motive. It opens the gate to that motive. And when that motive emerges just by itself as a happy mutation— an instance of what we saw in Chapter II of the good as self-realizing—it is bound to be confirmed by the advancing intelligence. Thus dawns the third stage, love.

So we have here the three stages stated in Chapter I. First in animal evolution came the power-motive, centered naturally on life's trend in each separate body to prolong itself there alone. As we have said, it was the main passageway for the entrance of evil. Nor, of course, has mankind quite closed the door to that today. The stages overlap. Then came the second stage, as the goods of life realize themselves more and more: intelligence. Notice now a point about this stage. It *included* the first stage and enlarged it. Intelligence gave its owner more power than he had before, knowledge of ways to get more goods, new goods. But more still, it had the trend just in itself to lead to the arrival of the third stage, the love-motive. And note again the factor of inclusion. The third stage with its cooperation gives more power for the group and for each individual therein to promote its needed goods, and more and more intelligence, not only for the joys of knowing as knowing, but also for the ways of discovering new ways to maximum good for each and all. The unity of the stages has increased; the second includes the first and helps the third and the third includes the first two.

The Temporal Expression Of The Divine Nature

But is this matter of the three stages really a *law?* Isn't it just a course of events that happened this way as the chance-mutations went on? Recall now what we said about its being a temporal analogy to the nature of the Divine Trinity, a temporal *expression,* however limited, we might say, of that nature—indeed what we would expect, since the effect surely *must* express the nature of the cause, the created minds in their development *must* show in their limited and analogous way the nature of the Divine Person, three in one. So now to see how this is the case. And that will enable us to see that it is truly a *law*.

We repeat for emphasis. In the Trinity, the First Person, called Father, signifies the Creator, God as power. The Son, Second Person, is the Word, *logos,* the *truths* as to the nature of the Creator and His relation to the creatures, showing mankind what they should do to approach Him, truths made clear by the Son to the *knowledge* of mankind. The Holy Spirit, Third Person, is the *uniting love* between Father and Son, God as *Love,* loving His children, leading them more and more to love one another. So appears the analogy in the temporal process of the three stages to the three Persons— Power, Intelligence, Love. Doesn't this look to guarantee the eventual realization to the full of love, the principle which as we have noted *unites* the power-motive and the rational, the intelligence-motive? If the effect *must* reveal the nature of the cause, must not the *law* of the three stages in the temporal creatures do what the nature of its cause implies, make evil sometime non-existent?

Further Empirical Evidence

Come now to another example of the law, confirming our claim that it holds of conscious mind's very nature. It is seen not only in the succession, evolution of mind after mind as time goes on, but in the individual conscious mind as it develops in its lifetime.

Yes, the law holds of the individual, when developed as in mankind's civilized life. Look at the three periods of his life: childhood, adolescence, maturity—their traits often overlapping of course, yet each with its predominant character. In childhood and early youth the main factor is activity, venture, playful exercise showing what the child can *do,* what he want to *do.* He likes to exercise his powers, jumping, running, throwing things, wrestling, competing with his comrades in his games. And this holds of his activities especially as they increase when he grows into youth. The healthy youth would show his power in fighting, winning in games. Note in passing that this holds typically more of the boy than the girl—as would be expected since he has more *muscle* than the girl, *muscle* the source of strength, power in acting. He values power more than she does, the power-motive being stronger in him lasts longer, continues into his maturity as it doesn't so much with her. Hence the typical contrast of the sexes throughout history—man the doer of big deeds, plain for all folk to see, the public figure, woman more the quiet one, exercising her powers over the male by her still beauty. As we shall see, she plays her part more effectively in the third stage to come, as the individual matures.

Now witness the second stage. As the child grows to adolescence in civilized life, education becomes prominent. He goes to school, learns to *know* more and more. Intelligence now often becomes the dominant motive, leading to the pursuit of knowledge for its own sake, as has occurred in the development of the scientist. See then how naturally comes in the stage of knowledge, how the *activity* of the individual leads right into the stage of learning, knowing, understanding, reason—activity now more of mind than body.

How do we come to know something of the real world about us? By *looking,* by exercising however slightly the *activity of attention.* When we are asleep we don't exercise that activity, not even in our dreams. When we wake up, it begins as we open our eyes—an act, even if involuntary. Then we become *aware* of things around us, and this awareness includes always some degree of *attention.* We *move* our eyes, *listen* with our ears, often moving our heads too with each, and knowledge of real things comes as a gift. A gift, yes, we don't create the external world. Even more is this activity present when we seek *new* knowledge, as in the sciences. Here is added the activity of thinking, trying to conjure up some new hypothesis to explain what happens. It has usually been believed that this effort, if we are fairly intelligent, itself produces the new hypothesis which "swims into our ken". But here as so often, the words of the poet show an insight deeper than this common view. Intellect, reason, *of itself* produces nothing! All it does is to attend to the present data, to what is known so far, opening its mind to a purely receptive attitude, hoping, looking eagerly here and there, wishing for new information, and then if it is fortunate *receiving* the suggestion which "swims into its ken" and looking further to see if it fits the facts so far known. Yes, this second stage follows and *includes* the first stage, adding to it by no creation of the first, rather by a *gift* from without, that gift due to an external agency, a *law* we must call it, always present in the life of intellect. Such has been the progress of the sciences.

True, the majority of mankind are not scientists, the scientist is a specialist. Yet the above holds of all, so far as they come to know more about reality, indeed anything about reality. We all learn by *doing,* acting physically or mentally. And note again what we stressed above in the matter of biological evolution—the fact of *inclusion* so far. The later stages of the law include the earlier, the progress is toward the unity of all three—the analogy of the temporal to the unity of the Trinity—as we shall see in the third stage of the individual.

Come then to the third stage in the normal typical human individual. As the second was a latent possibility which realized itself as the first continued, the like is true of the third. It is latent already in the growing early youth, steadily increasing in adolescence: the love-motive, seen first in sex-

love chiefly, leading to the family and family love, even from
that to love of one's group, clan, race, nation, as time goes on
in history. This third stage, note also, includes the first two,
even as the second stage includes the first—again analogous
to the Divine Trinity, the unity of the three Persons in One.
Family love—to go no further—includes the urge to activity
in earning one's living to provide for the family, to increase
the power to gain its needs by knowing more about the things
and persons one meets. And as with some the love-motive
grows broader these activities and this knowledge also grow
broader—to *help* more and more the needs of all and to
know the ways of so doing.

See now more specifically how this inclusiveness of the
third stage in the individual comes as if   inevitably in our
human nature. As said, our biological make-up drives us to
the family with its normal trait of family love, and with most
of us going little further. What then does family love *demand?*
The preservation and happiness, so far as possible, of the
family. And this requires work, typically, on the part of the
male as we just said, earning his living; on the part of the
woman, looking after his health and comfort, the like for the
children, the well-planned household. Notice here also what
we said above: the activity stage is seen more in public, more
outstandingly in the male, as he matures, than in the girl as
she matures. So this third stage, the love-motive, is typically
more prominent in the woman. The man's part has more of
public activity, his business, his profession. The woman's is
more centered on lovingly conducting the household, on love
of husband and children, caring for their individual welfare,
health and strength. Yet the man's work, while not so much
intensifying the love-motive, does in its own way *broaden* that
motive. How does the man usually, normally, earn his living?
By producing *goods* which others outside his family want and
need, and being rewarded by their paying him for what he

does, thereby enabling him to continue so doing. The farmer is rewarded for producing corn, beef, and such for his fellows; the grocer for giving his goods to the public; the carpenter for building and mending their houses; the plumber for putting right the flow of water they need; the teacher for instructing and training the youth; and above all the doctor and nurse for promoting the health of others. Isn't it striking that the individual's more or less self-centered life, less so in the family but still rather unmindful of much of the good of those outside, is actually conducted by providing for the *goods* of the latter? And when the intelligence of mankind increases as it is bound to do with his growing respect for knowledge, can he fail to see that all this points to a mutual-aid motive, to a universal love-motive? So this motive, dawning as the biological mutations move increasingly toward the goods of life, will surely commend itself more and more, including as it does the joys of creative activity and advancing knowledge, to the human individual.

Such then is the law of the three stages as empirically verified in normal civilized everyday individual human life. Come now to witness this law in an area of man's life of deepest import to his future, his religion.

Three Stages In Growing Religion

Growing, we say, for we here center attention on the three religions of the Mid-East and the West—Judaism, Islam, Christianity—rather than the perennial religions of the East, more static as they have been in the past—Vedanta, Taoism, Buddhism, for instance. True, these have changed to a degree as time went on, but the central motives aimed ever at just one goal, *escape* from the Wheel of Existence, the law of Karma, the vast complexity of human life and pain, to the timeless One. Not that we declare these religions all wrong, mistaken. They have their truths, as we have elsewhere affirmed, truths which need not conflict with ours which we can and should welcome. But the time element has till recently entered so little in their purview that we could hardly expect the three stages we are now to witness to be very prominent. Come then to see the three stages as occurring in the general trend through the above three religions of the Mid-East and West.

The earlier forms of religion preceding these with their many gods, even one supreme god, worshipped them as *powers* whose favor must be gained if mankind is to prosper, here or hereafter. Now and again sacrifices must be made to placate them. And when the above three monotheistic religions came, this motive continued. The one way for man to gain the bliss of heaven is to do the *Will,* to obey the *commands* of Almighty God. *"Thou shalt not. . . ."* "Who is the Lord of hosts? The Lord mighty in battle, He is the Lord of hosts." The Founder of Christianity, knowing what would appeal to the stage of development in his hearers, declared: "Fear not them who kill the body, rather fear Him Who can destroy both body and soul in hell." And Islam from its beginning has been a legalistic way of life with its commands by Allah to do thus and so in daily ritual or be lost. Not that this respect for God's power has vanished of late. As we said, the later stages include the earlier. And that brings us to the second stage.

Each religion claimed that itself alone is the one *true* religion, acceptance of its *doctrine* the one way to heaven. So entered the truth-motive, emphasis on the *creed,* as the second stage; second as it came later, after the religion had become a definite group, socially recognized, growing in influence, in power to get disciples. Now the disciple must *know* something of the Divine nature, must *state* as clearly as he can His way for the salvation of mankind. Witness especially the devolpment of Christianity with its stressing of the creeds, the *teachings* of the Church, the *knowledge* of what you must believe if you are to be saved. "I am the *way,* the *truth,* and the life" said Christ the incarnate *Second* Person of the Trinity. True, this was for the disciples then largely a matter of *faith* rather than reason. The intelligence-motive had not when the creeds were formulated progressed very much. But that motive had definitely entered, and it increased as the philosophers came in, not only in Christianity but in Judaism and Islam too—witness Avicenna, Averroes, Maimonides, Philo Judaeus—in the Christian Church later culminating in St. Thomas Aquinas.

Well, with this entrance and, as mankind's intelligence grows, the increase of the knowledge-motive, there would naturally come conflicts due to the inevitable difficulties confronting the limited human intellect in its "quest for certainty" about the Divine Being. At any rate, conflicts did come within the Christian fold, Christianity the dominating religion in Europe and the West, where intelligence has been on the whole more developed than elsewhere—as in the growth of the sciences. The outstanding fact here is that in Christianity there are more of the conflicting sects than in any other religion—as we noted above. Even so, see what is at last coming forth today: the love-motive earnestly seeking to abolish the fights between these sects with their differing creeds, as in the World Council of Churches and the recent urge to reconciliation by the Catholic Popes John and Paul. As the differences grew greater in this religion, the love-motive has grown stronger than in the past.

Whence then this motive? We said, it is central in Christianity from the first, in the teaching of the Founder, who emphasized it more than had yet been done in the religions. Yes, it came in as the seed of the third stage in the growth of religion, its *entering* on the scene. He, the Second Person, living the love-life as no man had yet done, brought into outstanding emphasis the third stage, the love-life. No longer is the righteous life induced by a stern "Thou shalt not", rather by a positive appeal to a feeling, a moving urge which our given human nature does value, acknowledge it or not—the love-motive, source of so many joys. "Thou shalt love the Lord thy God with all thy heart, with all thy mind, with all thy strength. And thou shalt love thy neighbor as thyself. On these two commandments hang all the law and the prophets." And Jesus announced that after leaving this world he would send the Holy Spirit, the Third Person, God as love. Such was the entry of the third stage in the long history of the religions, slow as it has been in getting emphasis in His churches. And note once more what we saw above: this third stage includes the first two. Jesus said of the Spirit: "he will guide you into all *truth.*" And he had already said: "I am the way, the truth, and the *life*"—life the *active* living, no mere matter of belief, of accepting the creed, *living* the love-motive even as he had lived it in his deeds of *power,* curing disease, feeding the multitude, and such. Yes, here entered and has grown with us the third stage in religion. Can we hesitate, after witnessing these stages in the evolution of life, in the individual person's life, and in religion, deepest of human concerns, to declare that it is a *law,* an inevitable course of progress?

Yet even if you admit that this third stage was brought into the light and emphasized by the Founder of the Christian religion more than by any other prophet of religion, even if you acknowledge that with us Christians today the love-motive has grown prominent in our urge to settle the quarrels between the many exclusive sects, you may well insist that this amounts to a very slight advance if you consider the extraordinary length of time, the 2000 years that have elapsed since Jesus lived and taught. To put it frankly, how little, how feeble has been the work of the Holy Spirit whom He promised to send! Surely the empirical evidence of history doesn't guarantee a third stage which is *bound* to increase, to do away with our evils sooner or later. Well, let us look at this objection.

An Objection Concerning This Third Stage

See how our human evils persisted in the Christian church itself *after* the Founder had taught the love-gospel, introducing this third stage, promising its development as the work of the Holy Spirit. The law of the three stages hasn't seemed to work very well in regard to the third stage. What of the martyrdoms, persecutions, up through the Middle Ages, the exclusions, the fights between the sects, still strong today? Above all, what of the *increasing* fights between nations today? Would the Holy Spirit, Third Person of Almighty God, move so slowly, so weakly? If in our claim of the *Law* of the three stages as shown in religion we are, as we declared, relying on empirical evidence, that evidence doesn't seem to confirm our claim. Notice, too, how little in the Christian creeds has the presence and the work of the Spirit been stressed. As we saw in *Rational Religion,* Chapter III, the churches for nigh two thousand years have centered their attention on the Second Person, Christ the Savior, reconciling us to God the Father if we would but accept his sacrifice on the Cross. To be sure, after all this lack of regard for the Holy Spirit, the love-motive, today at last some of our good theologians are telling us that we should focus attention on the Spirit. See the recent book by Henry P. Van Dusen, head of Union Theological Seminary, *Spirit, Son, and Father.* Yet how many centuries went by before this recognition of what Christ promised to send came forth. And if the Spirit, God as lover of all humanity, not of Christians alone, has worked so very slowly in the Christian churches, how much slower and lesser in public life outside them—see the increasing crimes, fights between races, groups, nations, more in the open than ever before. If this third stage, advent of the Holy Spirit in humanity, has accomplished so little in the long centuries since the Savior left this world, can it possibly have the force of a law?

Well, recall that He said nothing about when, about how quickly, how slowly, the Spirit would fulfill its mission. On the contrary He said: "Of times and seasons knoweth no man, save the Father only." Is a law less a law because it acts slowly? Think of the enormous length of the process of biological evolution. But of course the force of the objection lies in this: how could God the all-powerful, Divine love, the Holy Spirit, permit evil to have its way so very, very *long?* Doesn't it look as if the Divine love wasn't strong enough to fulfill its aim at least *reasonably* soon. It had, it would seem, to fight for ages upon ages against its foe, even if to win at long last.

True, we suggested above that this persistence of evil was due to man's free choice which was given him that he might overcome evil by *his own* work, giving him a merit of *his own,* not just by the work of the Holy Spirit. And then the objection came up: suppose some at least will always choose the evil deed—how then can there be a *law* which goes against, denies this gift of freedom? Isn't the work of the Spirit always liable to fail because of our free choice? Doesn't that choice imply that evil *can't* be overcome?

Well, this last objection *can* be met. The law does *not* exclude the presence of free choice. Rather it implies that as our intelligence increases, however slowly, we come to see the value of the love-motive more and more clearly, thereby the appeal of that motive grows stronger and stronger, so much so that our free choices will naturally be exercised less and less between the good and the evil deed, and more and more between goods which don't conflict with other goods. As we progress in seeing and feeling what are the deeper and more lasting goods and what are the more superficial and transient, then when they conflict we feel more strongly the lures of the former and the choice becomes easier. The more we advance in intelligence—the second stage!—the more we come to the third stage, the love-motive, and the less do we have to exercise our wills to do what is right. The deed as it were comes to do itself. Does the loving mother have to concentrate her will to feed the baby what it needs? She does it without any struggle, any effort. So does the choice between good and evil lessen, and wouldn't it naturally, eventually disappear? Did the poet go too far when he said:

> Vice is a monster of such hideous mien
> That to be hated needs but to be seen.

To be *seen*, yes, seen as what it really is, the frustration of some good that we need, want, should have as just a good in itself.

And as our civilization has advanced, our free choices *have* turned increasingly in this direction. Today, for instance, the average man is much more interested in games, sports, athletic contests, than in the past. They play a greater part in his life. He chooses more or less freely which to see, which to take part in, usually with no moral issue present. But just compare these games with those of the past—the gladiators, bull-fights, cock-fights, and such. To lose there was to be cruelly hurt, even killed. In our modern games the free choice of the player doesn't typically, normally, injure his rival. It is a joyous contest to both. Especially in the quiet social games such as cards, chess and others is this the case. If there is any morality at all in the matter it is this: be a good sport! *Don't* feel hurt by losing! Respect your opponent's freedom to choose as much as your own. There is no harmful conflict here.

But of course, you may say, this is but a trivial example.

Not much of our life can be spent that way, if we live properly. Indeed, aren't we doing too much of it today with our television sets, our demand for shorter hours to work, more and more done by our machines, our quest for more and more leisure? And anyway, even if what we have said about changing the direction of our free choices is right, and someday we shall have come to have no choices between conflicting goods, as they won't conflict—yes, even if the law of the three stages *will* sometime be fulfilled, there remains the objection about the extraordinary length of time. Indeed, if we look at our situation today, with its evils apparently *increasing,* the objection is strengthened. In our most advanced nations crime is on the increase. In Africa and Asia the newly made small nations are fighting more than when they were only colonies. And on the whole they have more opposition, more hatred of us than before. Added to this is our problem of the Negro, awakening to the injustice hitherto put on him, violently demanding his rights—more fighting by him than for years in our peace-loving nation. If anything, the love-motive seems rather to be dwindling, not only in the world at large, but even with us in the U. S. A.

Well, quite apart from this matter of time-length, which we shall take up in a moment, let us say now that we shall in our last chapter look at the empirical evidence concerning the alleged failures, the weakness of the love-motive in our third stage, and we shall find that evidence pointing decidedly the other way, to its prevailing more and more. As we are to see, our present world-situation is in the nature of a crisis, a critical point in its history, which will bring forth the love-motive with a new and greater energy than could have emerged without that critical point. But now to the time-length objection. It applies not only to Christian history but far more to the ages before that.

Why Evil So Very Long?

Life came into our world, we are told by the scientist, some millions of years ago, then conscious animal mind with its pains and death, and later still mankind with its wicked passions lasting even today. Why should the Perfect Lover have let evil continue for such an incredible length of time, not only in the past but doubtless in the future too, as we can't expect to overcome our human ills for many years to come, can we? Why didn't He have the course of evolution with its mutations toward intelligence and the love-motive go more quickly, its evils vanishing in a short time? Remember what Jesus said: "I saw Satan, like lightning, fall from heaven." Why didn't God do the like with the evils of the world? It isn't enough to answer that they lasted so long because mankind with their free choices *wouldn't* remove them. That might account for much of their persisting, but not for the slowness of evolution in earlier conscious minds, even in primitive man. For ages they were too weak, too ignorant, to overcome their evils. How long it was before intelligence dawned! Yes, the problem is: why so weak so long?

Well, you might offer the following as an answer. See how natural it was that evolution, as the advance to the increase of more and more good, would proceed slowly in the earlier stages of conscious mind. The evils of those earlier days persisted long; the goods of that time as compared with ours of today were slight. But so, too, were the evils. The sensitiveness of the lower forms to pain, for instance, were and are today small as compared with the like in us human beings. The long ages of animal life below man were ages of relatively slight evils. Even today in the higher forms below man, most of their life—as in ants, bees, birds, cats, dogs, horses, cows—is evidently not painful much of the time. They don't worry, fear, plan to injure others as do we humans. They seem to enjoy life except when hurt. And as the evils in these conscious minds below man's level were for ages so much less, the trend to remove them would naturally be less. Especially note this: these long enduring evils are much less impressive when we realize that they were not *felt* as long enduring by the animals or even by primitive man. Those conscious minds weren't at all concerned about the long past, only about the present and the immediate future. What disturbs us today about the long ages of evil didn't disturb them at all. Such then is the reason why the progress of evolution toward abolishing life's evils was so very slow.

There offers itself another reason for the great length of time. See what a vast distance there is between the experience of the earlier forms and the ideals of the good life as set forth in the Christian and other religions. Still vaster is that distance between this last and the non-living arena out of which evolution arose. What a terrific, well-nigh incomprehensible difference there is between non-living material things and conscious life, especially the human mind with outgoing love. Matter, having no good just in itself, must come to show itself capable of displaying all the grades of being up to mankind at its best. Could this be done quickly? Perhaps so, since the Creator has power unlimited. But would it have impressed late mankind viewing the past unless he realized the vastness of the development by seeing the tremendous length needed to produce it? Is there not something awe-inspiring when we contemplate the ages of ages from the earliest thick fog to the gradual condensing into definite bodies, then chemical combinations preparing for the entrance of life, then the evolution from simplest life to the incredibly manifold world population, man's mind with its spirit-urges at the summit? Doesn't it look reasonable that God would have proportioned the length of time to the magnificent accomplishment—at least the length of time as estimated by man's time-sense? For after all, aren't these millennia of slow evolution long only as compared with man's brief life?

Ah! these last sentences have revealed a slip in our proposal. Would we dare to say that God made the process so very, very slow and long just to waken tiny *man* to its teriffic accomplishment and future possibilities? Hardly that. No, we must put the matter in a quite different way. God made man so that to *his* time-sense, the process must when he is sufficiently advanced *appear to him* an incredibly vast production, a wondrous growth in the *values* of reality as time went slowly on. Well then, is this enormous time-length *really* so long as it seems to him? Aren't we estimating it from our little human point of view? Is our feeling of a time-length even in our common daily life always correct? How can we judge a *real* time-length quite apart from its bearing upon *any* connection with our human progress, coming as that has done from inanimate matter through earliest life-forms to conscious animal and at last to our present highest stage of intelligence and the growing love-motive?

How then, to repeat, can we estimate correctly the length of *objective* time, time as the sequence of events just by themselves, quite independent of any relation to our little human values? Well, let us turn to our physical sciences which surely seem to be doing this. They take a time-length as a definite quantity, a steady uniform succession of events, always going at the same pace, as in a good clock. Such was the Newtonian view, and it seems to be accepted today when they estimate the length of past time by the number of years—years and their parts, the hours, minutes, seconds always of the same length. Don't we measure daily time by the *uniform* motion of the clock's hands? Don't our senses tell us that one swing of the pendulum is just as fast as the next, until we see it gradually slow down and stop? We seem to observe directly, unmistakably, this instance of time going always at the same rate. And so, to come back to our problem above, we judge the presence of evil in our world to be terribly, cruelly long—many thousands, perhaps millions of years. Even if this wasn't felt by our ancestors, *we* feel it today.

Well, our claim will now be, wild as it must seem, that there is no proof whatever of time's steady pace as above declared; rather, its rate may be variable, what appears long may be short, and conversely.

A New View Of Time

Surely we should begin by looking at our common *experience* of time, since all our knowledge of the real world comes from our experience of that world. So let us dwell again on what we suggested about our ordinary everyday estimate of time-length, of time's pace.

Well, this common everyday life of ours experiences values, good and bad. When the value-phase is prominent the pace of time as we directly experience it certainly does seem to change. When, for instance, in the morning we are doing some work we highly enjoy, concentrating on the thing we are producing—the picture we are painting, the music we are composing, the problem whose solution we are finding and writing down—it suddenly occurs to us that we have an engagement at twelve o'clock and we look at our watch and find that it is five minutes to twelve. Time has raced by. As we look back at the morning's work we sense a kind of temporal bunching. The separateness of the successive steps as each occurred, then vanished, followed by the next, has obviously lessened. Time has condensed itself, shortened. We noted above how in the earliest ages, so far as is known, of the non-living universe, the picture was one of a vast cloud, a very thin fog, and how gradually through billions of years it condensed into units of matter, distinct bodies. See the analogy with our own temporal experience at the other extreme. Spatial being consolidates into unit bodies: time in the latest conscious minds now and again consolidates more or less into unit periods. Indeed, our psychologists have revealed the like on a much smaller scale in what is called the specious present. That present is a brief event here and now which includes a little of the past and a dawning of the future. It is, might we say, a quantum of time. Time in us moves by quanta, what Whitehead stressed in his doctrine of "actual occasions". And these quanta are often variable in extent. Sometimes the specious present is very brief, sometimes longer, according to our being bored or interested in what is going on.

But what, you ask, has this to do with the meaning of time as used by the physical scientist? Let us then look at the meaning of time for science. And here note a certain contrast between space and time. It is suggestive in this matter to compare our two organs which are most used in apprehending the external world, the eye and the ear.

Eye And Ear, Space And Time

The eye is more especially the space-organ, the ear more the time-organ. We see the extended world, we see its extent, and we see much of that at once. However we focus our gaze on a particular object, the eye senses the area around it, aware of that area as it extends itself indefinitely, more and more clearly seen as the object's distance is the greater, yet with no definite limit. There is a suggestion of the unlimited, the infinite, in our vision. As we look at the sky, we never see the end of space. It is as if we could travel on through space for endless years. On the other hand, the ear doesn't give a direct experience of such extendedness, while it does hear sounds in succession. Again, the eye sees the arrangement, the *order* of things in space; it is more akin to the intellect; the ear, as we are to note, is more akin to emotion. The eye, while of course it perceives the movements of things, sees them at once with its inclusive glance in the specious present. The ear doesn't sense the order of things all at once, that order is sensed gradually in time. The ear is more susceptible to emotion, as when the spoken words often appeal to our feelings. Especially there is for it music, which is on the whole, by and large, the most *moving* of the arts, the specially temporal art. Our everyday language suggests something of this: we speak of the mystic *vision* as quiet, contemplative, non-temporal; of the *voice* of conscience *moving* us to act in time, the *call* of duty likewise. The very *emotional* mystic Jacob Boehme spoke repeatedly of the heavenly music.

The eye is more active than the ear. Not only does it focus on the particular object, it can turn itself as the ear cannot. We turn our heads to hear something better, we do the like to see something more clearly, but we don't turn our ears. The higher animals can prick up and move the outer ear, but we can't do even that. With us the ear is a passive organ; so is the eye as it receives light-rays, but the eye is also active, self-moving. It is thereby the discoverer of much new *knowledge* of the external world. And what a vast panorama it views! The ear, being more receptive, is more *sensitive* to what is now going on, to what is just coming; the eye centers more on what *is,* what exists here and there. Sounds, the voices of our friends or foes, the growls, barks, mews of animals, the thunderclap, explosion, these have typically more of the emotional phase than the sights of the external world. We don't hope, usually, for the position of a satellite of Jupiter, we hope for *our* future, we regret *our* past. *Science depends far more on the activity of the eye than on the ear.* Religion depends more on the ear than the eye, as in the prophets' call, the sermon, the vocal prayer, above all on the hymns. Of course, all these contrasts are largely matters of degree, but they are there. Yes, the contrast of eye and ear in our human physique brings to light the distinction between the realms of fact and of value. Our very sense-organs stress it.

Would there be any values for us animals if there were no goals we *seek* to gain, no facts we *strive* to abolish or bring about? Even the motionless beauty of the landscape for the eye is something we want to *linger* with; the pleasant is what we want to continue, the painful to abolish. Values are for us temporal by and large. Time is *for us* primarily an affective-conative affair, space just a factual being. So then do our feelings influence time-length, as we noted above. When things are monotonous, change slight, we are bored, time drags. When we are doing the work we love, time condenses itself. Time is for us the value-category *par excellence*. Its speed, its length, depend for us conscious beings on its value-traits.

But you say, this applies only to *subjective* time, to our feelings about time-length. What about *real* time, time as it goes on in the external world, *objective* time, not at all in the conscious minds, time having nothing to do with good or evil? It would seem that time as it goes on in the space-world must be quiet different from our subjective time-experience.

We said just now, in comparing eye and ear, that the sciences depend on the eye far more than on the ear. And the eye is especially the revealer of space and things in space, even moving things in space. *So science naturally tends to think of all these given facts in spatial terms*. Now space gives *quantities*, wholes made up of parts, all parts equally present, thereby constituting the whole. Lengths, areas, volumes, these all are definite quantities. Precision of knowledge about them involves measurement. And as precision of knowledge is the goal of science, the laws which science discovers must be stated in quantitative terms. Hence the central place of mathematics, mathematics built as it is on timeless logical implication, as for example in the geometry of our three-dimensioned space. Yes, for science all must be conceived in terms of definite quantities. The motion of a body, its distance covered, and the time occupied therein, must be described in those terms. Objective time is conceived in spatial terms—as a *line,* straight and long. One time-length must be *equal* to some other, or if longer or shorter then by a definite amount. Time must be measurable precisely. If the force which moves a certain body unhampered is equal to another force later moving that same body unhampered, the motions must be equal—the same distance covered in *the same length of time.* This means that time proceeds always at the same pace. So we think of time as a straight line, having one dimension of its own as compared with the three of space. Yes, the scientist thinks of time in terms of spatial properties. And thereby does he not miss the value-potentialities of time, potentialities which come out in the open when conscious minds arrive? Didn't Bergson see this meaning of time when he declared that the scientist's treatment of time in spatial terms overlooked the true essence of it, the note of increase, growth, progress to the greater and better?

All the same, you may reply, this time as experienced by conscious beings with its evils and goods went on in the regular succession of days, years, centuries, quite indifferent to the feelings of these beings. Do you think *your feelings* about the velocity of the earth as it goes on its elliptical orbit around the sun, could make the slightest difference in that velocity? And as that past history of our planet was very very long, so was the succession of evils when conscious minds arrived also very long—just count the years, the centuries since then. So we return to the same objection: why did God let the time be so terribly long?

But now pause and reflect. Have we, in noting above the scientist's conception of time as a straight *line,* divisible into definite parts succeeding one after another, each a precise quantity—have we examined this conception enough? No, we reply. It needs further analysis. Come then to it. And here is our pivotal heresy!

Objective Time-Length—Not A Precise Quantity

A time-length, you say, is like a line in space, and therefore we can measure it as we measure that. But now see the difference. The line in space is all there, every bit of it, none disappearing while we measure it. That is not so with time. The past isn't here—how can you measure what isn't here? A quantity is a sum of parts, all equally present in the whole. If some parts were lacking, the quantity would be less than it is. In an objective time-length all the parts are lacking except the present moment. Time *cannot* be a definite quantity! Why then, you ask, have our measurements of time been successful in fitting our conduct to the stream of events? Surely we have to treat each minute, each hour, as equal in length to every other. We couldn't be sure as we are that the sun will rise tomorrow at six o'clock unless tomorrow's six o'clock is just as far from today's six o'clock as today's six o'clock is from yesterday's. We couldn't predict *when* something will occur unless *when* means just so far from *now*.

No, time-lengths don't have to be equal. It might be the case that *everything* in the external world slowed down today and speeded up tomorrow. So long as the events therein *kept in step* with one another, we wouldn't notice the difference. If two men walk together, each keeping step with the other, there is no implication that the successive steps continue the same in length or speed. We judge the time-length of a process by comparing that length with a *number* of events which we *assume* to go at uniform speed. We say the lecture took just thirty minutes because the minute-hand of the clock moved over thirty equal spaces on the clock's face. But there is no proof whatever that it moved at the same rate in each step.

To be sure, as we look at each step it *seems* to go at the same pace as the earlier ones. But that only means that *our feeling* of the time-lapse in each one, *our* time-sense, keeps the same pace with each. It might well be that our feeling of time itself also slowed down or speeded up, we not knowing it. If we assume that there is a real objective time, as indeed we must and our science does, we have absolutely no proof that it goes on always at the same rate. Time, the source of change, may itself change. All we need to accept is that in the course of events each event goes always at the same rate *as compared with other events then occurring.* And so, as we calculate the time when event *A* will occur, we mean only that *A* will occur when the hands of the clock *B* will have revolved a certain *number* of times. Nothing is implied about the length of each time-unit. We take some one particular series of events as the standard by which we estimate the length of all other series. In our everyday life that standard is the clock. For the physical scientist, especially the astronomer, it is the speed of light, always the same, as Einstein *postulated* in the theory of special relativity. Notice, however, that we state the velocity of light *also* in terms of our clocks—some 186,000 miles *per second.* Of course this is justified pragmatically, as are all our scientific discoveries; it enables us to predict with success *when* something will occur, in terms of our clock-revolutions in the last analysis. For we measure years by months, months by days, days by hours, hours by minutes, minutes by seconds. And as we said, we think the clocks go at the same rate because our time-sense usually seems to do so. But there is no possible proof that real time doesn't change its pace. On the contrary, there is a strong suggestion that it may, as we have pointed out. Our own time-rate, when concerned with our work rather than the outer world, does change. When we are happily busy it is shorter than the clock-hands would declare; when we are idle or bored by monotony it is longer than they would say. If this holds of one set of events—mental events—why shouldn't it hold of some other set—physical events?

How then can we assert that the ages of ages of our universe's history are really as long as they now look to us? We measure them in terms of our brief lives. Suppose we lived each a thousand years, or even a million years, how much shorter would we judge those ages. Consider the example of the little short-lived buzzing fly in our houses. Its wings vibrate with—to us—an almost incredible rapidity. Here is a fly on your desk. You try to kill it, you slap down on it quickly with your hand. As a rule, the fly easily dodges the blow. It looks as if the motion of your hand, to you so quick, is to the fly *slow,* slow enough to let it see the place where the hand starts, the direction in which it is moving, the possible ways of escape by flying in this or that direction. Surely time to the fly goes far more slowly than to us. Might there not be beings to whom the incredibly long ages of our universe would be as brief compared to our time as ours is brief compared to that of the insect? Who knows? We on our little earth have no sight of such beings, but some of our religious ones might affirm that the spirit-world contains them, angels they would be called. And these Christians would declare that this increase in time-speed reaches its consummation in God, the Timeless One, to Whom all time is present at once. We recalled above that Josiah Royce put the thing in terms not so far from our human experience when he suggested that in God time is an infinitely long specious present.

No, let us repeat: time has *of itself* no fixed steady pace. This goes with what we saw above: time is not a definite quantity. When we measure it we compare the *number* of events of this or that kind with the *number* of events which we take as the standard. But those unit-events which we take as the standard have themselves no fixed time-length, no fixed value as ultimate quantities of time. If time were a definite quantity that wouldn't be the case. The absence of past events prevents us from seeing how they can combine with the present as a definite quantity of time-length. Space has its quantity, and we think we measure time by the space travelled by a body in uniform motion, where uniform motion means that for *our* time-sense there is no speeding up or slowing down. But for other time-senses than ours there might be such. Time has *in itself* no fixed rate, no fixed numerical value. It has, indeed, one trait of quantity; it is more or less, longer or shorter. But the amount is not a necessarily fixed amount. For us conscious feeling minds, its length varies, for the non-living it has no definite length in itself.

To be sure, we might say truthfully that life arose on our earth some two or three millions of years ago, provided the earth was then revolving as now about the sun. But what would a year mean before the origin of the solar system? Where is the common denominator by which to compare it with the events in that system? And what would be the meaning of time-length before light came on the scene? Was there always light? Even if it came to have a constant velocity by which to measure length of time, how could time-length be measurable before its arrival?

Of course all this is not to deny that time *could* go at a steady pace. We have seen only that it *need* not, and that our experience of values, our feelings of good and bad, of delightful work and of boredom, *do* show an actual difference of time's rate. It might well be that events in our space-world are now going at a fairly steady pace; but it doesn't follow that they always did in the past or even will in the future. Our whole point is just this: the objection to a solution of the problem of evil which stressed the long continuation of evil rather than the speedy overcoming of it, has no basis, no *logical* ground, and may be dismissed. And all the more may it be dismissed when we recall what we said above, that our *feeling* of the long continuance of evil didn't come forth in the long ages prior to the dawning of the religions. It was these religions, especially Christianity with its stress on the love-motive, that woke us up to realize how far we have been and still are, with our failures to live that motive, from abolishing our evils. Only within the last two thousand years or so, short as that period is compared with the age-long primitive life preceding it, did this *feeling* of evil's terribly long presence emerge. An evil that isn't felt isn't an evil! Our *consciousness* of the long continuance of evil, which means its being an evil for us, is not at all a matter of the great length of time preceding it.

No, the real difficulty in solving the problem of evil is this: is there solid ground for affirming that someday all evil *will* disappear, be *unreal* as the past is unreal, all pain abolished due to the work of conscious beings—a situation analogous, as we said above, to woman's experience in childbirth, stressed by the Founder of Christianity. This was indeed declared in the Bible at the end of the book of Revelation. But what we the defenders of reason in religion need is to show that the empirical evidence of history looks well-nigh to guarantee this. That evidence we give in Chapter VII.

Well, let us now bring to light a certain motive, long inherent in the life of animal and mankind, and today coming more and more into prominence especially in the latter—a motive which in itself points in that direction. It is what might be called the play-impulse, though its significance, as we are to see, is far above that trivial quality so often associated with play. We spoke of it above when we discussed the matter of free choice being exercised less between the good and bad, and of late, as in our sports, more between goods that don't conflict. But it has hitherto scarcely been recognized to be as fundamental in life as we shall find it to be. Yes, it deserves more respect than it has had. It merits investigation. Come then to the next chapter on the significance of this impulse, this motive, for the goods of life. It points in the direction of the vanishing of all evil, even if it gives no strict evidence.

In fact, as regards the answer we have offered to the problem of evil, even if the empirical evidence supports strongly the law of the three stages which, we have claimed, should imply the final disappearance of evil, no rigid proof as to the future can be given. No, not even in physical science which leads us to accept without question certain predictions of the future, for instance, that the winter will follow the summer and autumn which have just gone by—even here there is no absolute proof as in mathematics. But at least one strong point in the answer we have offered is that it cannot be *refuted,* referring as it does to the future. And if it does answer the question *why* God permitted evil by showing how that not only *could* make for a better world, as it would make the creatures better, stronger, wiser, more loving due to *their* work, than they could be without evil, if it *also* finds evidence of a *law* of three stages which expresses, as the effect *must* express, the cause, then surely the argument seems strong indeed. But now to see how the play-motive has itself urged the progress of mankind through the three stages.

CHAPTER VI

THE PLAY MOTIVE

What is the nature, the meaning of this moving impulse we call play? What is it, to play? Look at some typical examples which we commonly call play. Children play, adults play games, authors write plays. Perhaps we can best see what is common to these by noting their contrast to the serious moral life.

Serious, we said, as the essence of morality appears in the old phrases "Thou Shalt" or more often "Thou shalt not". It is a command, an *order to do* this or that, or to *refrain* from doing this or that. If you do the right, you have merit, if you don't, you have blame. You are responsible for what you choose to do. In play there is no such stern command, no responsibility giving a sense of guilt if you do wrong. Witness the happy play of children. They play because they want to, no inhibitions. They enjoy its free activity just for its own sake, it is good just in itself. And we want them to play! The like holds with adults when they play their games, quiet games like chess, poker, bridge, or strenuous athletic games, football, baseball, races, etc. In these games the element of guilt has no part so long as you follow the rules and don't cheat. Cheating is wrong because it isn't *playing the game*—be a good sport! It isn't wicked to beat your opponent, there is no sin in his beating you by his superior skill. There is a freedom quite apart from any responsible choice, and it is normally, typically, a joyous activity *for its own sake,* as in the play of children. So it is with the dramatist who writes a play. It is for him a joyous creation, an activity he loves for its own sake, a product of his genial imagination, no compulsory description of fact as for the truth-loving scientist. It is a scene to be *played* on the stage, not realized in the outside world. Those who portray it are the *players,* they *act* the imagined scene which the eager author conjured up in the joyful exercise of his mind.

Exercise, we say, for that is central in play. Children's play is bodily activity—running, jumping, rolling on the ground, climbing a tree, throwing a ball—just for the delight of doing it. They may do it alone, they may do it in a group—racing, wrestling, etc.—the latter especially in the boys with their growing physical muscles more than in the girls. And as the children grow their activity becomes more social, as in their games—hide-and-seek and such. Yet always it is *doing* something, however slight, a doing focused on the pleasant, the joyful—no feeling of something they *ought* to do, of the difference between right and wrong. And the same is present in the games of the adult. There is a freedom quite apart, as we just said, from any feeling of responsibility, of blame or merit. You can play any card you wish, move your pawn where you choose—subject of course to the rules of the game, itself a purely pleasant activity. In the quiet games you don't exercise your muscles, but you do exercise your thought. The motive of joyous activity is present here as much as it was when you were a little child.

And surely we do respect this motive even in our advanced civilization with its increasing sense of the right and the wrong, of the basic need of the moral life in our society with its many, many crimes. Witness the crowds today at the baseball, the football and other public games. Yes, we feel that the play-motive has a goodness of its own, even if sometimes it is misdirected, even if it doesn't look to have anything morally good in it, just a drawing away from the deep concern we *ought* to feel with the grave troubles of mankind and the

serious earnest work that demands of us. But let us now see
something of what this goodness is.

A Goodness In Play

Yes, we must admit that play is a withdrawing from the
toilsome arena of our social life where we do—at least should
do—what work we can for the good of our fellows, to some
easy activity, easy because pleasant, joyful, a retreat from labors which the truly conscientious one feels demanded of him.
True, this doesn't apply to the play of children, in whom the
moral sense has hardly dawned as yet. But it does apply to
the grownups. Isn't it then just a self-centered thing, seeking
your own pleasure, indifferent to the pressing needs of your
brothers and sisters? We all condemn the emperor Nero because he *played* music while Rome was burning.

But look again. The moral life taken with utmost seriousness, is toilsome, exacting, exhausting. If it demands that we
must *never* cease in our efforts to help our fellows, it defeats
itself—we would die of exhaustion. Morality itself commands
you to stop now and then and *rest,* rest to renew your strength
to go on working. Without rest you couldn't continue your
good work. You must relax! You must respect yourself and
your powers if you are to use those powers to help mankind.
Well, there is where comes in the good of the play-impulse.
The quiet games with your friends in your home give you
that joyful easy activity that diverts your mind from the social troubles and renews your strength. Likewise, this holds
when you witness public games, when you take part in the
social dance, and go to the theatre to see a play. Generally
speaking, play is that which restores your strength to do the
creative work for the good of others. *Recreation is re-creation.*
It gives you the power *to create again,* to produce what you
should, what the moral law requires of you. It is the moral

holiday which gives you renewed strength to come back to work.

And there is another good, working in the same direction, essential also to the very nature of play. In the game, your opponent, your rival, is your *friendly* enemy. There is equal opportunity with you both, each respects the choice of the other to do what he will as much as his own. It is the spirit of *fair play*. It is precisely the same spirit as the moral law commands in your dealings with other people in the practical business of everyday life. Equal opportunity for all, to each according to his needs!

Yes, play rightly conducted, no cheating, no bad feeling toward the rival, ministers to the moral life. And on the other hand, as we saw, the moral life itself ministers to the joys of play, so natural to our human make-up, just because it *needs* them, *requires* them, to restore the strength which it must have if it is to go on. See then the polarity between the two. Each ministers to the other, helps the other to be, to continue, and each is a good just in itself. And each is deep in our human nature—there is nothing haphazard, nothing trivial in either. If the play-impulse emerges in early child-life, it doesn't vanish later when the moral law comes in with maturity, since that moral law demands its counterpart, the playful joy of the game. We must *retain* that joy, contributed by the life of the little child. Isn't that perhaps why Jesus said: "Except ye become as little children, ye shall in no wise enter the kingdom of heaven"? Anyway, it *agrees* with what he said.

An Objection

Yet here comes an objection, one often felt by the earnest moralist. Look again at the happy play of childhood. Often there is the note of just *fun,* as we might call it. How often does the child laugh happily, joyously! And we adults, often enough, withdrawn from the cares of the day's work, join with our friends, say, in a happy evening together, not even playing a game, just conversing with wit and humor, joking, laughing—all quite in the spirit of the child's happy laughter. We are having fun—and with fun goes the *funny,* the laughable. Well, might not the serious-minded Christian object to all this as frivolous, idle time-wasting? Even the game is serious while played. Surely, he feels, the Christian gospel finds no room for joking, humor, laughter. Let the child laugh happily, but the adult should outgrow that phase of play. Recall the words of St. Paul: "When I was a child I thought as a child, I spoke as a child, I acted as a child. . . but when I became a man I put away childish things." As one of our highly respected professors used to say to his classes in Ethics: "There is no recorded laugh in the Gospels from the lips of our Lord." Is there any evidence at all that Christ ever laughed? Have our Christian churches with their creeds taken any notice whatever of laughter? No, says the objector, it is all right for us now and then to play games; they relieve us from the carking cares of exhausting work. But we shouldn't go to the *extreme* opposite of serious work, laughter as good in itself.

Laughter As A Good

But now see the meaning of our laughter today as contrasted with what it meant in the past. In the old days, even up to today with some, laughter was *derision.* They laughed *at* a person as ridiculous, absurd, a fool. Laughter was ridicule, scornful. So it was in the days of Jesus. Recall the instance related in the Gospels, of the behavior of the Pharisees toward him: "and they laughed him to scorn." Surely he would not wish his disciples to laugh at any one that way. Least of all would he have done it himself. No wonder that there is no recorded laugh from him!

Well, how different is the friendly laughter we *enjoy* today in our social gatherings. That laughter is typically not *against* a person, even if to some degree at his expense. He doesn't resent it, he can laugh at himself. The spirit of the good sport, as in the games, is present as it scarcely was in the past. Even more, our humor, our jokes, are more impersonal than before. We conjure up stories full of fun, we enjoy comedy on the stage far more than tragedy—comedy with its laugh-provoking scenes. Even in the most serious of social meetings, at the church on Sunday, there is hardly a sermon today that hasn't some witty jest, the congregation responding with audible laughter. See, too, that all this social humor, this laughing *together,* makes us *like* our company, works in its own way to grow the love-motive. The fun-motive, as we may call it, leads here right into, enters into, the fullest life of all, the love-motive, essence of the moral life which is true religion. It should *not* be excluded, it should play its part in the genuine religious life. As a woman of unusual insight in this matter has written "The 'religious' attitude toward life is that of wholesome, honest fun as well as of serious duty" (Georgia Harkness, *Conflicts in Religious Thought,* New York, Harper & Brothers, 1949, page 20). Yes, fun has its proper place in the good life. See also the last chapter in the book *God* by John Elof Boodin, entitled "Divine Laughter".

A Needed Warning

Proper, we said, for there is of course a danger here, a danger hovering indeed over our cultivating any kind of play, but more prominent in the light-hearted joys of wit and humor, laughter. Especially is this so today with our worries and troubles over threats of world-war, increasing crimes, and so on. As these troubles are felt more than ever before, as we are the more distracted, the more are we driven to the extreme, to withdraw and comfort ourselves with those joys calling for less and less exertion, doing what we naturally like just because we like it—our cocktail parties with their easy fun, our demand for shorter and shorter work-hours, increasing pay that we may have more of these idle pleasures, and such. Yes, there is always the danger of carrying the play-motive too far, especially that form of it which doesn't even use as much exertion as playing a game, the lure of immediate pleasure here and now as in watching television, no sense of its consequences, its bearing on the rest of life. Isn't this why the strict moralists have always condemned the search for happiness, always condemned hedonism? Well, if they have gone to one extreme, the play-motive in this easy-going form tends so naturally toward the other extreme, and we do have to watch it! Never must the latter be carried so far as to exclude its polar counterpart, the hard-working labors of work for the good of all. Yes, we do, many of us, today need this warning. When as today so much of our hard work is done by our machines, there is a growing trend toward too much easy pleasure—*too much* television, for example. The play-motive tends with many to become a threat! We must be acutely aware of the polarity of play and work.

Well, so far as to a goodness in the play-motive, one without which most of us humans couldn't *be* good, couldn't go on living the life we should. But there is much more good contributed by that motive, as we are now to see. Seldom if ever has this been recognized; it has given rise to much, very much, of the progress of mankind through the centuries, progress in the individual and in society.

Play-Motive Giving Progress

To begin with, look at what the child's play brings forth. It is to him a delightful activity, at first just by himself, before the social element comes in, playing with other children. It is exercising his muscles, his powers. He tries many ways, well-nigh all possible ways open to him, of exercising them. And thereby he *learns* new *truth*. He finds out what he can safely do, what he had better *not* do. He comes to realize however slowly that there are external powers which he must respect—thus enters his sense of the real external world. If he didn't do this playful activity, he wouldn't become aware of the forces which give that world its reality. We humans don't become aware of external reality by first using our intellects, by reasoning. We become conscious of its reality in our early childhood by the experimental acts which make us feel that we have to heed its powers. When the child bumps into a tree he learns that there is something there!

Come now to the next childhood stage, where his play is not only of the individual alone, but extends itself to the group, however small. Here enters the game. Of course these stages overlap in childhood, even later, but on the whole the games with their more or less order, their rules, get more attention as the child grows into youth, teen-age, maturity. The game is social, and being social must have some order of its own. It couldn't go on if the individual player could do just anything he pleased. So comes in, however faintly at first, the motive of adapting your play to the play of *others,* so that the joys of play may go on without hindering the joy of the game. Consideration for others enters the scene, others who behave like you, who *are* like you, other *selves.* You couldn't go on with your games, to which the play-motive has led you, without being aware of the reality of other selves.

So then as to the contribution of the play-motive to the growth, the progress to maturity of the child: he learns first by his individual play, a free activity as it is, about external things, then later he learns by playing with others to respect their ways, he becomes aware of *persons* as individuals like himself. It is through *playing* with others that he steps beyond the region of his own impulses and realizes that there are other selves. He can't help believing in them any more than he can help believing in the real external world. Notice that here lies the cure of that philosopher's *virus,* solipsism. We all believe in the external world, real just by itself, and other selves present therein, not because we can prove it by reasoning, but because as living acting beings we just can't help it. And it is that play-impulse which in our young life brought this about. Let us then respect it more than has been done!

Recall now what we said above of the *law of the three stages* in the progress of conscious mind. The first stage, centered on activity, has been viewed just now in relation to the play-impulse. Come then to see what it contributes to the development of the second stage, centered on the realm of intellect, reason.

Play-Motive Helping Pure Knowledge

Yes, this motive has given mankind knowledge of deeply important principles, truths, laws, which without it would scarcely have been discovered. After all, why did science come on the scene and grow and grow to its present height and majesty? From pure love of knowledge just for its own sake, not even from the desire to help our fellows. Of course we are speaking not of the practical science of medicine but of the pure-knowledge sciences such as physics, mathematics, and astronomy. With these latter that desire to help mankind did come in later when they gave many discoveries which were very helpful in improving man's daily life, and it has grown stronger and stronger. But it was not the originating motive, and even today it isn't the *leading* motive. That motive meant retiring from the moral, the religious demand for practical action to better the human lot, still less to guarantee a blessed after-life in heaven, retiring to play the joyous game of discovering new truth, a joy quite by itself, let the cares of the world go by! Game, we said, for a game has its rules, and science has its strict rules. Indeed, the rigors of scientific method

are so strict—minute observation and measurement, every suggestion tested by experiment, by rigid logical implication—
that we now tend to think of science as rather a moral pursuit,
quite the opposite of a game. Even so, the motive command-
ing these strict rules is pure joyous discovery of new truth, just
for its own sake.

See now an instance of scientific discovery which helps to
confirm the claim we make concerning the contribution of the
game, of play, to our increasing knowledge. Look at the
betting games—betting on horse-races, roulette, on winning
at the card games, and such. Taken so often by the stern moralist as degrading, the plain fact is that from such idle games
of chance has been discovered a principle of maximum import in science today. It is the notion of probability, of chance
in the modern sense, seen in the principle of statistical law.
Were it not for man's indulging in these petty plays, this
would hardly have come into the light. As it was, the mathe-
ical mind, noting the facts brought out in these games, conceived the calculus of probability, and the empirical scientist
came to verify its presence in the statistical laws of nature.
It was a great and fruitful novelty. No respect for such a principle, for chance in any sense, had been hitherto held even by
the scientist. Order, rigid order alone, was his ideal. Yes, these
petty little games have given us their weighty contribution. Is
it not a delightful irony that this notion of chance, despised
and rejected of man the intellectual, has in our most advanced
science, physics, come into its own through the door of the
least respected of our human activities, betting on the unknown future.

Such then is the contribution of the play-motive to the
second of the three stages in our human progress, the stage
of intellect. See now its gift toward the development, the increasing presence and influence, of the third stage, the love-
motive. Not, to be sure, that it has yet explicitly proclaimed

and urged that motive; only that it has moved decidedly in that direction. Distinct as it still is from the genuine morality which is the fulfillment of the love-urge, it has furnished a motive which of itself moves toward that fulfillment. This contribution is seen in the realm of the arts, their beauty and thrill.

Play In The Arts

Recall the meaning of play as defined above. Play is doing something just because we like it, no ulterior motive, no feeling of ought or ought not. We saw that the scientist works for the joy of discovering new truth, of understanding why this or that is so, just to satisfy an inborn intellectual craving, no other motive at work so far. Later reflection may convince him that he ought to do this, that it is a serious duty to cultivate intelligence, understanding, reason. But it wasn't this that started him. It was just the *felt* good of knowing, knowing what is and why it is. That is part of the make-up of the human mind as it naturally develops in the course of evolution, a native impulse, just as native as the play of children, though as the individual grows up it may conflict with other impulses and he may or may not choose to gratify it. Well, the like is true of what we dub the artistic motive, love of the beautiful, the stirring and thrilling, as in the lovely flower, the sweet smell of the rose, the taste of the food you like, the sunset's colors—not only does the child enjoy these, he wants them to come again, to continue. As he grows up he feels the impulse to produce, to make them occur as far as he can. He has the creative impulse to make things he likes to see—he builds a little house out of the mud, whittles the wood into a tiny boat, and so on, all done out of pure joy in creating the liked, the lovely, the beautiful, the thrilling to look upon. And all this is in the spirit of pure play, nothing more as yet. It is precisely what moves the adult when he creates a work of art. Other motives may come in also—he may want to make what will please his fellows, what will give him fame, even what will strengthen the moral urge in others. But the one original moving force is the playful urge to make the lovely, the beautiful, the stirring thing. Emotion dominates, opens the door to the third stage.

True, there are two kinds of artistic production, the practical work of the artisan, making things useful to others, and the fine arts, typically of no direct practical use, so called. Look then first at the work of the artisan.

Play In The Artisan

Consider some common everyday examples. Doesn't the shoe-repairer want to do a good job, to mend a shoe carefully, thoroughly? He *likes* to see that he has done it well. The seamstress, the dressmaker, these *like* to see that they have sewed the cloth firmly, have constructed a pretty dress. They seek the joy of a job *well done*. Of course this may be only a part of their urge to make what they like to make. They want to earn their living by pleasing their customers; that may indeed be their main motive. Yet there is to some degree also a delight, a pure joy in making some good of its kind. They choose, so far as they are free to do so, the kind of good they like. It is so far the same motive as that of the athlete who would run a good race, the chess-player who would play a first-rate game. The difference of the artisan from the gamester is only in this: the artisan produces what is directly useful, the player's action isn't guided by that aim, though it may, as we said, result in his better health, his keener intellectual processes, his renewed strength for the serious work of daily life. But come now to the fine arts, a realm so long and widely and carefully studied by our thinkers, past and present, and so little hitherto considered in any relation to the play-motive.

Play In The Fine Arts

As we just said, the play-motive has in general been given little regard and respect by the earnest thinkers who would portray to us the ideal goods to be pursued by us human beings. And as the aesthetic realm, the fine arts, have given us many of these, they have been taken as good of themselves, in their own right, so far akin to the goods of the moral life. What then can they have to do with the petty pleasures of irresponsible play?

On the contrary, we declare, the play-motive is, if we are open-minded, quite obvious here, even more so than in the scientific arena. Take the example of the music composer. He loves to compose music just for its native beauty—a case of art for art's sake, not for the sake of anything else. He plays with music. He conjures up this melody, that melody, this harmony, that harmony, this combination of both, that combination. He has no sense of responsibility except responsibility to produce what gives the joys of beauty. As the gamester is responsible only to the extent of playing by his game's rules, so it is with the musician. As the gamester is free to make many moves, so the musician is free to choose what pleases him with its beauty, and there are many such choices open to him. How very many are the beautiful examples of music, even by a single composer! To be sure, here as with the artisan, other motives may come in. The writer of beautiful hymns may have the religious urge to convert the hearer, but he loves their beauty too, as deeply moving. Indeed, isn't music more moving as a rule than any other art toward the love-motive—witness the wide appeal of the hymn, the love-song, the rhythmic sway of its music in the friendly heart-warming social dance? But this doesn't at all exclude, rather it helps the lure of the beautiful chords and airs which draws the musical genius to journey to and fro at his own will, playing with all the possible combinations coming to his mind, choosing the ones he likes. Isn't that why we speak of the performer as *playing* his instrument?

And much the same is true of the other fine arts. The architect would plan the well-ordered, most beautifully structured building out of all such possibles he conceives. Of course here, as with the musician, other motives may enter: witness the cathedral in the form of the cross, the Gothic spire pointing to heaven above, stressing the religious urge. Yet the play-motive, choosing what will, out of the many possibles occurring to him, best gratify his urge to create, to produce the beautiful, the romantic, the thrilling—this delightful activity of his mind is the basic moving force. And isn't this obviously the case with the other fine arts—with the sculptor, poet, novelist, with all indeed? Each plays his beloved game so as to play it best, to him a joy in itself, art for art's sake again. The entering of other motives—art for more than art's sake—may and does occur, but it doesn't at all rule out the originating impulse of art for its own sake.

And let us in passing note one more delightful irony, this time in connection with the art of drama. Don't we respect personality as the very highest grade of being? Don't we Christians—also Islam and Judaism—believe in a personal God? Whence then came to us this conception? From the drama, the *play* acted out on the stage, even centuries ago. The Latin word *persona* meant the mask through which the actor spoke, playing his special part in the drama. It distinguished him from the other actors—hence it came later to denote an individual, a separate human being, a person. Yes, the notion was first suggested, originated, in the play-arena. A *person* was a *player!* Would we ever have come to use this word, at first just a *dramatis persona,* to denote a being to whom is due the maximum reverence, love, dutiful obedience, without this playful contribution from the art of drama?

An Objection

But now comes a protest against our claim of the play-motive's high contribution in the fine arts. What can there possibly be in common between a majestic cathedral, Beethoven's magnificent Ninth Symphony, and a wrestling match, a boat-race, even less in a trivial game of poker? How could these lofty, awe-inspiring works of art be in the slightest degree a matter of irresponsible play? Perhaps the play-motive in art does seem present today when the surrealist, the expressionist, gives us all sorts of drawings, paintings, music, in which most of us can see little or nothing of beauty, of fine taste, of any meaning at all. It does look as if these modern artists are just playing a game to amuse themselves. But surely nothing like that is the case with the great classics. They were produced in all seriousness, nothing light-hearted about them, no irresponsible freedom to produce what they happen to like. What could be more serious than Bach's Mass in B minor with its deeply religious feeling? How perfectly ridiculous, absurd, even wicked, to put it in the same class with a game of poker!

But now see: it is not in connection with its *results* for the high uplift of mankind to contemplate the great, the magnificent, that the kinship lies between these extremes. It is in the matter of the originating motive, the joyous exercise of an activity *for its own sake,* be that activity one that will result in the uplift of mankind, be it only one that will win a game you are playing. It is the *direction* of that activity that counts. The basic moving force, delight in active doing, is alike in all. That delight need not exclude the noblest of motives *also*—the joy of doing what will in the end bring about the greatest possible good to all mankind, the love-motive.

And here is the outstanding point in this arena of the arts. We noted that the play-motive in the work of the scientist brought in what we have named the second stage, second of the three stages we affirmed in the evolution, the progress of conscious minds, of us human beings. Well, the arena of the arts leads *toward,* to a degree however slight usually, realizes *something* of that third stage, which we saw as the fulfilling of the love-motive in active and intelligent living. Love, as we have insisted, includes knowledge and action, it is the *moving* urge, the *motive* which realizes the third stage. *Emotion* it is, *emergence* into *motion,* action. And in the fine arts, emotion is above all prominent. They stir us, move us—such is the nature of beauty, of the thrill of a romantic episode, as in a novel or a drama. The hymns awake us to long for the good, the righteous life. Even the games, quiet as in chess, active as with the athlete, give us a sense of good fellowship, of fair play, as we said. The social dance likewise, with the joy of a partnership, however brief, between man and woman, often leading to and confirming a true love between them. Yes, the fine arts do lead us, have led us, into the third stage of our human progress. And in their highest, most appealing forms, they have pointed to the religious life, as in the great classics—the love-life.

See finally how this play-motive, hitherto so neglected, or if noticed then scorned, does in the third stage eventually *unite* with the sincere and earnest moral life, so commonly taken as its eternally necessary opponent.

In proportion as mankind grows in the moral life is the union between the playful joys of doing something that feels good and the moral demands more nearly approached. In the fullest development of the moral life, however far from us that now is, one does the righteous deed not from any stern dictate of conscience, but because he loves to do it. It is a pleasure, a joy in itself, there is nothing hard about it. Recall what Jesus, the Perfect Moralist, said to his disciples: "Take my yoke upon you, for my yoke is easy and my burden is light." The ideal love-life is the life of joyous morality, of doing many kinds of things you love to do, of experimenting too, to find new ways of doing such things. And there is a freedom here which is not present in the earlier stage where no choice is offered as to what is the righteous deed. That stage is the stage of conflict, struggle, the hard way, painful self-sacrifice often demanded, this one deed the only one permitted. But as we have more and more of the love-motive, we seek and find more and more ways of helping one another and we freely choose between them, none forbidden, yet this or that one selected as the one we *prefer*, like better than the others, is under no external compulsion as in the rigid moral law. It is the play-motive as in the child, delightful activity a joy in itself, as it has evolved into the second and third stages, has discovered the joys of knowledge and of love as including both knowledge and action. No wonder that Jesus told us to become as little children!

And it is significant here to note, as we said above, that of late this play-impulse has been recognized by some as present in the Creator. The earlier doctrine of the Vedantist, taking this world, Maya, as illusion, has been replaced by the affirmation that God created the world in the spirit of joyful play —a delightful free exercise of His activity. Why then shouldn't we Christians have such a view? Surely, believing as we do that He freely created this world rather than many others He might have made, and that His perfection implies fullest love and joy, wouldn't His creating be a most joyful activity, all the more so as it increases that joy as He exercises His love toward the imperfect and needy creatures? And to accept this is to see more of the analogy between our limited imperfect lives and the Divine nature. It is an added example of that analogy, and it goes to account for the presence and the deep significance of the play-impulse which we have been pointing out above.

Well, has this study of the play-motive and its function as

promoting the goods of life, a study revealing, we hope, more of the trend to increase those goods than we would otherwise have noticed—has this study given evidence enough of that final triumph of the love-motive in the third stage, in the future development of living conscious minds? Not quite enough, it seems. We want empirical evidence based on the long course of history, and especially on the world-situation today. Especially, we say, for this situation on the face of it today hardly supports so hopeful a belief. Evils, increasing crimes, wars, hot and cold, increasing in number in the new young nations just released from colonialism—all these are in the highlight, headlined in our newspapers and journals. Yes, we need greatly such *empirical* evidence of our claim that the third stage is *bound* someday to be realized more and more. Come then to this evidence in our final chapter.

CHAPTER VII

THE BRIGHTER OUTLOOK

Here we shall not only see the strong positive evidence for such an outlook, but shall also look at the prominent evils of today and find that they do not at all deny this positive evidence, rather, they tend to confirm it.

So now we first bring out concrete empirical evidence that the love-motive has through the centuries not only widely and deeply increased, but is today steadily growing much more than appears on the surface of things. In spite of the grave troubles that confront us and make many despair of the future there is a strong and growing undercurrent—and not much beneath the surface either—which points to a brighter outlook. But let the reader be prepared for pages filled with dull statistics; they are a necessity for the consoling conclusion to which they lead. And we must begin by being quite clear as to what love means—repeating as usual what we have already said.

Love's Meaning

Well, the word *love* is commonly used to apply to quite different situations. Can it mean the same in all of them? Hardly, it would seem. Does sex-love mean the same to most of us as the Christian brotherly love? Does love of God as in the First Commandment mean the same as love of music, of knowledge, of painting, drama, and other forms of beauty? Does self-love use the word in the same sense as love of the neighbor? Is *eros,* is *philia,* the same as *agapé?* The fact is, that there have been all too few attempts to be clear as to love's meaning. Of course you may say it is just a matter of the way in which we choose to define it. This is true indeed. But our point is this: *not only* does the sense in which we here use the term reveal good empirical evidence for the hopeful outlook we are defending. At the same time it is a proper definition because it states what is common to the examples above, however they seem to differ on the surface. As Rufus Jones said, there are not different kinds of love, there is just love! "Men wrongly divide love into two types, 'human love' and 'divine love', but in reality there is only love" (*The Inner Life,* New York, Macmillan, 1916, p. 43).

To repeat our definition then: Love is the felt urge, carried out so far as can be done without injury, to realize most fully the potentialities inherent in the loved being. To be sure, there are *degrees* to which we may feel this urge. We may feel its urge strongly, or but slightly. But so far as we do feel it, just so far do we have the urge to have the loved one realize them. The love-principle itself is that positive urge to the fullest possible realization. And often we do feel this, perhaps hardly aware that we do. Yes, when we deeply love a person, we do really want that person to have the richest and fullest life possible to him or her. When we so love an animal, we want all the needs and capacities of that animal gratified. When we so love a tree, or other plant, we want it to go on living at its best—we cultivate it, as we say. If you dearly love your house and garden, you try to make them as beautiful and useful as can be. When we love a work of art, a picture, statue, symphony, we want to keep that picture, statue, music from being destroyed or lost, to keep it as complete and lovely as it was when the artist made it, with all its potential values to be realized by the beholder. When we love our work, we try to do that work with maximum fulfillment of its possibilities, to do it as well as we can, where *well* means *fully.* When we love ourselves with a genuine love—as indeed we should, being ourselves God's children—we want ourselves to become as fully developed in strength, intelligence, usefulness to others, and such, as we can. True, self-love is ambition in the good sense of the term, not just the desire for fame or power, but the desire to be great in every possible way—so far, of course, as it hurts no one else, rather helps each one. In sum, as says E. W. Sinnott in his book quoted above, speaking of the morally right: it is "whatever helps to realize the possibilities of life most fully" (p. 153) and that is "love, that benign affection. . .which helps to realize the possibilities of life most fully" (p. 154). And in line with our present thesis let us add "Love is the climax of all goal-seeking, protoplasm's final consummation" (p. 155).

To be sure, this word love, when defined at all, has more often been defined as the urge to *union* with the beloved. Certainly that holds of sex-love, friendship, love of beautiful things we want to keep with us, indeed of about all the common meanings of the word. Doesn't it hold, too, of the mystic's endeavor to be one with his God? Does it then hold of our love of those who don't happen to be our friends, whom we don't even know personally yet long to help? Indeed it does. Our definition doesn't exclude this one, rather it implies the same. To love someone whom you don't like or don't know, which is to work to do what will help to realize his or her potentialities, is to *put yourself in his or her place,* to identify yourself so far with the needs and goods of that person. You are yourself doing what his or her potencies call for, and to that degree you are uniting yourself with that other self. And this is true of everything you really love—human, animal, object of beauty, whatever it may be. You are striving to preserve and fulfill what the nature of the beloved object wants for its fullest development. To love the beloved one for his, her, its own sake is to love him, her, it, *"as thyself"*. There is so far no separation in this love, there is union, yet a union which respects the beloved as just itself too. Sameness does *not* contradict difference! Still, it is the practical motive of *helping* another that unites and so far identifies you with him, her, it. If we think of love as *merely* the urge to union, it is all too easy for most of us to interpret union as *being with* in the fleshly body. Love is then confused with liking, a common confusion, as we have above said. And perhaps with some of the mystics it may have meant *only* the desire to be absorbed in the Divine, forgetting that to be one with Him is to be filled with His love of all creatures and to act accordingly.

Yes, to love God Himself, as the great religions have commanded, is to do our utmost to fulfill in His creatures His loving purpose to give them the fullest being which their nature allows. To love God is to love His love, to do our part with the powers He has given us to realize His loving designs for His children. It is not, as some mystics have taught, *merely* to sense His presence in overwhelming bliss, though it does include that. God is love, and to feel His presence is to be filled with His love, with the overpowering urge to realize at the maximum the potencies of all His creatures, no conflicts between them.

In fact, love as here defined is an example of what Professor Arthur Lovejoy in his epochal book, *The Great Chain of Being,* called the principle of plenitude—fullest realization of all possibilities, no conflicts, no exclusions. Love is that principle embodied in the behavior of conscious beings. We stressed this above in Chapter IV.

Now to see how this love has slowly, gradually, athwart many terrific obstacles, emerged into the light of common day, as the most promising agent of a blessed future life; a life not only in heaven, but here on earth and in the flesh.

How Old Cruelties Have Disappeared

If we take a long overall view of man's progress through

the ages, what do we see? We see a tremendous gain in the love-motive. Not only have the cruelties so widely practiced by our forefathers slowly disappeared, sympathy for our suffering fellows has increased greatly and is today increasing at a quicker pace. As regards the cruelties, see the detailed account of their lessening in the book by Alexander Sutherland, *The Origin and Growth of the Moral Instinct,* (New York, London, Longmans, Green and Company, 1898). Take an outstanding example: punishments inflicted in the past on the criminal, the heretic, the socially condemned, as compared with those of today. Even in the Middle Ages there was burning at the stake; the rack, thumb-screw and other tortures still survived. Crucifixion was a thing of the past; hanging came to replace burning and beheading—a less painful death apparently. Now the electric chair has taken the place of hanging—a death which at least *looks* painless. Lifelong solitary confinement we have abolished. Yes, cruelty has definitely grown less; sympathy with the criminal is increasing. And what of the kindly souls who would abolish capital punishment? Quite a number of our citizens condemn the old view of punishment as a just retribution and would substitute a warm-hearted reformation of the criminal's character. Well, they may be leaning over backward, so to speak, but they are moved deeply by the love-urge. As we have remarked, love at its full demands correct judgment; it may be misdirected at first. But it must be first of all the moving force, the starting power. And surely we have arrived at that stage today as regards punishment. Recall, too, how in the 19th century badly behaving pupils in our primary schools were punished by whipping, and today no such punishment is permitted. Again doubtless love misdirected, but the love-*motive* has grown.

In Politics

In the political field, see the rise of Democracy. Whatever its weaknesses, corruptions, isn't it the emergence of neighbor love in that field? Equal opportunity, liberty, equality before the law, fraternity; "don't break heads, count them". Even the materialist-atheist Communism was designed to save the "underprivileged". And the like of other socialist planning. How many of these schemes do we find in the early centuries? Yes, even in our latest wars, hot and cold, we may trace the entrance of the love-motive. The Nazis didn't seem to have much of it, if any—except for themselves. They wanted to gain power over the world for their own race, the superior race. Fortunately they were defeated. Then came the U. S. S. R., hoping and planning also to conquer the world, yet with a motive the Nazis didn't have; they believed that their way of life, if adopted the world over, would save mankind from the evils of poverty, class-conflict, and such, so prominent in capitalism. True, they have been so sure that this is right that they wouldn't permit any other view to be entertained in their own domain. They resorted to force, they suppressed freedom of the individual to think for himself. Thereby, the love-urge became, we might say, love enforced, the individual's value found only as a member of the community, the perfect State. He is of no value as just himself. Yet while we who believe in Democracy cannot but believe this a mistake, we do overlook the fact that the love-motive did come in with the U. S. S. R. as it did not with the Nazis—however misdirected we believe it to be. Surely this was hardly the case with mankind's previous wars, due as they were to power-seeking, fighting against oppression, and the like. Today we are fighting, we may fairly say, to establish the rule of love throughout mankind—but the views of love conflict! And yet with this, we all desire peace the world over as

never before, owing to the terrific power of destruction which
the scientists have unearthed for us in the atomic bomb. We
think it was a terrible misfortune that the scientists did this,
but wasn't it really a great good, since it has led us to craving
for universal peace—surely a big factor in the love-motive?
And our Communist foes want it as much as we do. See then
how we are struggling today in the U. S. A. to gain some
agreement on ways of preventing war. Yes, contrary to what
seems so evident on the surface, the love-motive is working
within us as never before. And it is striking to notice that the
scientists, quite apart from any professed love-motive, are
working in the same direction. There is no hate-motive in
science. It is just love of knowledge, and especially cooperation in gaining that knowledge. So the scientists are more
and more meeting together, scientists from many different
nations, hostile and friendly nations alike, brightening the
spirit of friendly cooperation between those who before the
prominence of science would have remained bitter enemies.
And what is it that has brought on this spirit? The love-motive *so far*: love of knowledge for its own sake, all possible
knowledge of the world about us and in us.

Anyone who reads the two prominent journals of our scientists in the U. S. A., *Science* and *The Bulletin of the Atomic
Scientists,* will verify what we have just said. Some—by no
means all, far from that—of our religious devotees say that
science works against religion, denies the supernatural, leads
to materialism. Let these earnest ones realize that the scientists are showing in their *behavior* today more of the love-
urge than many of our professed religious ones. After all, their
discovery of the atomic bomb did two big things for humanity.
In the first place, it gave us victory. Bad as it was in killing
hundreds at Hiroshima and Nagasaki, it stopped the war
which would have gone on killing thousands. And secondly,
as we just said, it made us all so fearful of future wars that

it brought into the light as never before the urge for peace and harmony throughout mankind. Yes, the scientists have, however unwittingly at first, contributed greatly to the love-motive, more than many good Christians, professing the love-commandment, have begun to realize.

But of course that commandment is being more and more carried out in other ways, and we need to stress the fact. Look then at some of these ways. Here we consider mostly what has occurred in the U. S. A., though we begin with the work of the United Nations which is most striking.

Recent Foreign Aid

To quote: "The humanitarian activities of the U. N. have a particular appeal to Americans. A relief program in war-torn Korea saved an estimated 8 million lives. This program included the distribution of food, clothing, and other necessities and medical measures to avert major epidemics. Recent U. N. activities in the field of health have included tuberculosis and malaria control projects in Southeastern Europe, Asia, and South America. Medical personnel and supplies have been sent promptly to many parts of the world where they were urgently needed, and emergency relief measures have been undertaken. . .in areas devastated by earthquakes, floods and other disasters." (K. T. Hart, *Visualized Problems of American Democracy,* New York, Oxford Book Co., 1953, pp. 358-9).

See now the contribution made by the government of the U. S. A. We quote from the *Bulletin of the Atomic Scientists,* December, 1956, page 385, referring to the government's urge that our citizens help it to send food in packages marked CARE, Chicago. The statement is headed STARVATION. It says: "More than half a million refugees in Hong Kong face starvation. Teeming refugee masses have so congested the area that as many as 30 people live in one room, with no more than chalk lines to mark their 'homes', according to representatives there. Welfare checks show that 95% of the adult refugees have tuberculosis. Without any means of support, they desperately need food. U. S. government surplus food comprises the newest CARE packages. These packages, which may be sent for $1 each, will consist of 10 pounds of rice, 5 pounds of beans, and 4-½ pounds of milk powder (18 liquid quarts). Each dollar donated covers cost of packaging and distributing one package within Hong Kong. Each parcel bears the name of the donor, and a guarantee of delivery."

This is but one instance. We all know that our government has done more to help the struggling peoples of the world than any other nation in the past—and not in the sacred name of religion, but just to help the needy. The *New York Herald Tribune* of July 6, 1957, printed this: "Washington, D. C., July 5. The government reported today that foreign aid outlays totaled $1,250,000,000 in the first three months of this year. The quarterly figure brought to nearly $59,000,-000,000 total payments and deliveries of goods and services by the government to foreign nations since World War II. The Commerce Department said foreign aid in the first three months of 1957 ran 30 per cent ahead of the final two quarters of last year."

What we have just said was written in 1957. Hear now the statement in *U. S. News and World Report,* January 8, 1962, pages 29-30. The love-motive has been growing! "Aid given by U. S. to other countries of the world had passed 101 billion dollars at the start of 1962. That is for the period from mid-1945 to date. The 101 billion will rise above 106 billion in the year ahead. . . . The world has no other record of generosity on the part of one country to other countries even approaching that of the U. S." Shall we give details? See then, "Yugoslavia's Marshall Tito, a Communist dictator, has been given 2.4

billion dollars. This includes 700 million dollars in military aid. Marshall Tito is down for more aid. India's Nehru has had 2.8 billion dollars of aid. Nehru is assured of another big slice, even after his attack on Portugal's Goa. Communist Poland has been given 900 million dollars. It wants more. Egypt's Nasser, while engaging in intrigue against U. S. allies, has had 600 millions. He, too, wants more. Indonesia's Sukarno, who follows a Communist line, and who now is threatening to grab property of the Netherlands, a U. S. ally, has received 700 millions in aid. He is down for more. . . . Out of the 101 billions in total aid given by U. S. in postwar years, all of the nations of Latin America have been given just 5.3 billions. This compares with 47.3 billions given to Western Europe, with 16.2 billions to the Middle East, South Asia and Africa, with 23.1 billions given to the Far East and Pacific Area. . . . Today, Latin America and Africa below the Sahara—other than South Africa, Portuguese possessions and Rhodesia—are the great new areas for expanding foreign aid. . . . Foreign aid is divided into military and economic aid. Economic aid over the years has mounted up to 71 billions and military aid, 30 billions. Of this, Western Europe's share of 47.3 billions breaks down into 15.2 billions for military and 32.1 billions for economic aid. . . . Japan has been given 5.1 billion dollars. . . . Two thirds of that money was for economic aid. . . . Countries of Southeast Asia have taken 7.6 billions in aid. The Philippines, with 1.6 billions in aid and more in war-damage payments, has been put back on its feet. South Vietnam and Laos have been given 2.5 billions since 1954 in an effort to forestall communist take-overs. Thailand has gotten 600 millions." And we may add this comment: "Russia, with a record of aid that adds up to a tiny fraction of the U. S. A. effort, is considered by many in Congress to be getting far more for its money. United States officials administering aid, on the other hand, maintain that much has been achieved.

Development has been helped throughout the free world, they point out. Money has gone to feed the hungry, build factories and schools." And recall the quotation we gave from this journal as to the amount the U. S. A. gave in 1964—more than ever before.

True, no doubt, our motive has been also to bring these nations to our side against Russia. But that isn't the whole motive. We do want these people to develop themselves, to be free to do so; we do believe that they should be given whatever will help them in that direction. We do respect them as of worth in themselves. And that *is* the love-motive: to realize all the potentialities latent in the beloved object. And that motive *has* been carried out in the worldwide area, *has* been put into action, whether or not it will have the desired result, to an extent never before seen in human history.

True, it may be, as some critics have said, that some of this work has been misdirected, They say that we haven't adapted our gifts to the status of the receivers. Too much have we given them which they are not advanced enough to appreciate and use—machines too complicated, science-teaching too refined and difficult to understand, and such. Even so, the love-motive has emerged into action, and as we learn more about the undeveloped ones we shall direct it better and better. But come now to some striking examples outside the political field.

In The Social Arena

Listen to what President Nathan Pusey of Harvard has told us in his Report for 1960-61 about the work of that University's School of Public Health—work which surely cannot be attributed to any hope of gain against Communism. He says of the School: "24 members also participated for at least brief periods of time in activities outside the United

States, in Canada and the Caribbean, in eleven countries in Latin America, in sixteen in Europe; in Senegal, Liberia, Ghana, and the Ivory Coast in Africa; in Turkey, Lebanon, Israel and Saudi Arabia in the Middle East, and in India, Thailand, and Taiwan. There are now approximately 600 alumni of the School engaged in public health work in 85 countries.

"The School provided a setting in the summer of 1960 for a meeting of 81 delegates representing 56 corporations having activities in tropical areas in The Fourth Annual Conference of the Industrial Council for Tropical Public Health to discuss the responsibilities of government, industry and labor for health services in developing areas, along with such specific health problems as schistosomiasis, trachoma, poliomyelitis, influenza, newly discovered viruses, and insect control.

"On my recent trip to the East I saw much evidence of the valuable work this School has done in training public health officers and also of the high respect there accorded to it. I was especially happy to visit the Indian village of Narangwal, near Ludhiana, where a member of the School's faculty, Dr. Carl E. Taylor is spending this year with his family studying possible ways to bring the influence of medical science more effectively to bear on village communities in India. Dr. Taylor had earlier had a part in the population study carried on in the Punjab region by the School in cooperation with the Government of India and the Ludhiana Christian Medical College. . . . This sampling of new international activities, engendered by a changed world situation, must serve to illustrate the University's increased concern for peoples, cultures, and activities to which formerly we paid small if any attention.

"Last summer the University helped to prepare a group of young people for the Peace Corps who, after further training at University College in Ibadan, are now about to take up teaching duties in Western Nigeria.

"The Dean of the Graduate School of Public Health says in his report that his School's attention is increasingly focused on 'the unfolding panorama of health problems in international affairs'."

We have already in a previous chapter emphasized the significance of the Peace Corps. Could a finer example be given of the spirit of brotherly love?

Some Particular Cases

Now for a significant example within our own area. Toward the end of June, 1957, a terrible hurricane and tidal wave devastated parts of Louisiana, Texas, and farther north. We quote from the *New York Herald Tribune,* front page, June 30, 1957. Some "40,000 Lose Their Homes In Louisiana. 150 to 211 Dead. Doctors Fly In. Eisenhower Speeds Hurricane Aid, Makes Fund Appeal for Red Cross. . . Army units battled disease with water purification units. The bodies of the dead were stacked in an icehouse in Cameron as a sanitation measure. Soldiers and civilians alike battled deadly snakes infesting swamps and marshes. Eight helicopters shuttled medical officers and supplies from Fort Polk, Leesville, La., to the Lake Charles-Cameron area." From the same page: "President Eisenhower. . . gravely concerned about the suffering: 1. Declared hurricane-stricken areas of Texas and Louisiana eligible for aid from Federal disaster funds. . . . 3. Urged all Americans to contribute to the Red Cross. . . . Mr. Eisenhower himself made an additional contribution to the Red Cross this morning." From page 2: "More than 3,000 cots and blankets were sent in, along with emergency baby delivery kits and medical supplies. . . . The storm area swarmed with boats and helicopters, picking up the last of the hurricane's refugees and finding an occasional body. . . . The storm-lashed Cameron courthouse, one of the few buildings that suffered only minor damage, was turned into an emergency hospital. More than 1,000 rescue workers—soldiers, airmen, Coast Guardsmen and civilians—were working today at Cameron, which served as a collection point for the whole area."

We needn't hesitate to say that such warm-hearted help would not have been given 100 years ago.

Here is another example of much less publicity—we all tend to overlook what isn't in the big public eye—of our Christian love in the U. S. A., by a church to be sure, but with much lay assistance. We quote from the *New Haven Register, Sunday Magazine,* June 23, 1957, pp. 1-2. It concerns "28 young men and two women who face a future of freedom and opportunity in America after escaping from terrorism and death in their native Hungary last November. The Hungarian Refugee Relief Program of St. John's Episcopal Church, North Haven, has been a dramatic demonstration of how church people in an American community can put Christianity to work in a practical way. . . . St. John's is but one church among many in Connecticut and in other parts of the country which are helping Hungarian freedom fighters to start new lives in America. . . . In just about six months since their arrival these young people (in North Haven) ranging in ages from 16 to 28, have all made a good start on their new careers, either by going to school or college or by taking full-time jobs at area factories and offices. . . . Many are still living in North Haven as more or less permanent members of their new households and are regarded with great affection by their foster parents. One of them testifies: "I never imagined people could be so happy as they are in America. . . . Now I know freedom is more than a slogan in America." Also, "Besse-Richey Co. (New Haven) outfitted the first 12 (refugees) with clothing without charge. Sears Roebuck contributed bicycles. Doctors and dentists in the community gave them free examinations and polio shots to start them off on their new life in good health. . . . Classes were set up eventually for over 50 Hungarians in this area at Yale, at the St. John's Parish House, and at several high schools (to teach them English). These classes are still continuing and gradually the Hungarians are becoming more and more fluent in their new language. . . . In addition to the $1200 raised by the church (St. John's) that first Sunday, $1000 was contributed by Yale students and $500 by the International Rescue Committee. Total spending on the program has been over $4000."

Think also of the American couples returning from Korea with adopted Chinese and Japanese children. We have been blinded to this spread of good feeling among the common people by the wars, hot and cold, the crimes, the fatalities by car and plane, so prominent before the public eye.

We said, we are limiting our evidence mainly to the U. S. A. But we cannot neglect one most impressive instance from India: the work of Mahatma Gandhi. Here was an example of true Christian love by one who was not a professed Christian. We quote from E. A. Burtt's *Man Seeks the Divine* (New York, Harper & Brothers, 1957). "What did he find to be the heart of the message taught by all the great religions. . .? First, that love (implying an unqualified refusal to harm others) is the true way of life, the way to be uncompromisingly practiced by all who dare to believe it, come what may" (p. 484). "Gandhi was convinced, in brief, that love is. . . the effective force behind a dynamic problem of social reform" (p. 485). Professor Burtt notes the work of his disciple Vinoba Bhave "who has already persuaded the well-to-do landowners to part with several million acres of their possessions for the sake of landless peasants" (p. 496). "Under the leadership of Manilal Gandhi, son of the Mahatma, natives and Indians in South Africa have been organized in nonviolent protest against the segregation program of the South African government. General Rondon in Brazil, with a group of assistants trained in the Gandhian way, has succeeded in removing the hostile fear felt by the Indian tribes in the Matto Grosso jungles, so that they have been pacified and won to willing cooperation with those who are ready to teach them the arts of civilized culture" (p. 498). Such instances "may well mark the most significant development of religion in our time —a development in which self-giving love proves its divine reality and its creative power not merely in the spiritual transformation of individuals but also in the moral regeneration of society. Perhaps it will save the civilized world from suicide through a hydrogen war" (p. 499). In this connection, see the book, *Human Relations and International Obligations,* a Report of the Unesco-Indian Philosophical Congress Symposium held at Ceylon, December, 1954. (N. A. Nikam, Mysore University, Mysore, India, 1956).

We need only refer to one more prominent instance in the U. S. A., the recent movement against segregation of the Negro, alike in social and individual affairs, in the schools particularly, but also in hotels, restaurants, clubs, etc. True, it has given rise to new trouble—violence in some groups of Negroes, fighting, punishment by the police—their new freedom has stimulated them to excesses; they are not yet adjusted to it. But that adjusting is bound to come.

How much better Christians are these modern altruists, humanists, even atheists, many quite outside the Christian fold, than our Puritan fathers who thundered forth their sermons on the fearful torments of hell, sermons filled with sadistic detail! Talk about the "acids of modernity"—well, this unassuming kindly Christian compassion is the *alkali* of modernity. As Canon Streeter has said, "many an atheist is a better follower of Jesus Christ than some church-goers who proclaim their belief in the Trinity, the Atonement, the Virgin Birth, Resurrection, etc." Another Canon of the Anglican Church has written: "orthodoxy is not Christianity, nor is theology religion. . . assent to propositions about God, rather than godliness of character, became the condition of salvation in His church." (Charles E. Raven, *Jesus and the Gospel of Love,* London, Hodder and Stoughton, 1931, p. 24). He goes on: "Religion is life; and the quality of it can only be expressed by living," (p. 28). And "there are signs. . . that Jesus is exerting an authority far beyond the limits of the churches" (p. 32). We repeat: did not Jesus himself declare: "By their fruits ye shall know them"?

Think of the enormous advances in medicine—medicine which we might well call physical brotherly love. Think also of the numbers of women nurses today, as compared with the past. And the clinics, the Alcoholics Anonymous, psychiatrists, the faith-healers in one religious sect or another, all are increasing in number today—seen especially in the Christian Scientists, in the work of Oral Roberts and T. L. Osborn, in the new section of the hospitals for "retarded children". Then there is the modern "emancipation of women". Think of what women had to go through in past history! Today they have become leaders in charitable work as never before, they have started new religious movements—witness Mary Baker Eddy, Helen Blavatsky, Miss Farmer, Annie Besant. And not only in the Western world, but in the East of late is woman given more and more respect and freedom. We are told that polygamy in Islam is gradually disappearing—see *Islam and the Modern Age* by Ilsa Lichtenstadter (New York, Bookman Associates, 1958). And speaking of women as charity-workers reminds us of the enormous number of these kindly organizations in the U. S. A. Few of us realize their extent and the loving work they do. Just listen to the following names—we enumerate them that the reader may be impressed by their numbers. And there are many more than these. Here is the list: The Society for the Prevention of Cruelty to Children, another for Prevention of Cruelty to Animals, the Red Cross, the Blue Cross, the Amvets National Service Foundation, the March of Dimes (to help polio cases), the American Foundation for the Blind, the National Braille Press (for the blind), the Disabled American Veterans, the Boys' Athletic League (to lessen youthful delinquency), Boys' Town of the Desert (same motive), Boys' Town of Missouri (same), Girls' Vacation Fund, Guiding Eyes for the Blind, the Connecticut Humane Society, the Boy Scouts, the Girl Scouts, the Brownies, the Cub Scouts, the Sister Kenney Foundation, the National Wildlife Federation (to save plant and animal life), the School Settlement Association, Father Flanagan's Boys' Home, Berkshire Industrial Farm, Newington Home and Hospital for Crippled Children, Connecticut Child Welfare Association, Yale Institute of Human Relations, Piney Woods School (for Negroes in the south), Laurenberg Institute (for the same), Save the Children Federation, World Health Association, the Society for Social Responsibility in Science—and so on. We might even go into the high hundreds if we included the many, many local organizations the country over. Let us end this list then with the Salvation Army which, whatever you may think of its religious creed, has for many years done increasingly great and effective work among the poor.

Isn't this string of names fairly tiresome to read? But that only shows how most of us have little idea of the extent of the love-work going on around us.

Note, too, that it is not only the "middle class" who have founded these institutions. Today, in the U. S. A., the rich, the great capitalists, have done much. Witness the Rockefeller Foundation, the Carnegie Foundation, and others. In 1957, 84 institutions in New York City got $6,600,000 from the Wollman Foundation; among these the Bellevue Medical Center received $1,000,000 for a children's pavilion at the

New York University Hospital; Lenox Hill Hospital $1,000,-000; Mount Sinai Hospital $1,000,000, Barnard College $600,000; Montefiore $200,000; Maimonides Hospital $250,-000—to name but a few. For the first time in history, at least to a noticeable degree, the capitalist class is swayed by the love-motive.

Now recall what we said in Chapter VI about the play-motive. As a particular example of its contribution toward the progress of the love-motive—here is our last instance before we go to the religious arena—and from a field hitherto scarcely considered in this light, the field of athletic games. Bob Kiphuth, swimming coach at Yale University, talked the other day about the Olympic Games at Melbourne, Australia, of which he was a witness. (Precise reference is not here at hand, as the talk wasn't printed—but here is what he told us.) At the finish line of one of the track races an American Negro, a white American from the South, and a Russian met and embraced one another in warm friendship. After another race all the spectators—about 110,000—rose and applauded the winning Russian. And all the combatants and others met most cordially at the dinner after the games. Also, the Russian track coach and American track coach avowed that they hoped to meet again under more friendly relations between the two nations.

Yes, sport with its supposed fighting spirit has today a strong element of the love-urge. Just compare our modern sports with the old gladiator fights, the bull-fights, the bear-baitings, cock-fights, and such cruelties! We spoke above of science as enlarging and deepening the love-motive; the like is true of sports today. These two realms, apparently having nothing to do with morality or religion, have given and are giving more and more to that motive which is the center of the Christian religion. How many of us realize this?

Growth In Religion

Now for the great emergence of love in the religious arena. Of course, the Christian has ever proclaimed the love-gospel; what is new is its increasing *activity*. Recall the recent emphasis on the "social gospel"—the promoting of welfare in the everyday lives of our fellows, as compared with the older trend to think chiefly of going to heaven after we die. But not only in the practical field has religious interest increased. It has of late also sought new ways of approach to the Divine, ways which will—so it is claimed—if pursued renovate *our earthly life, body and spirit alike*. These new ways are the revelations of new sects. Do you realize how the number of Christian sects has in the last decades increased? And of sects not predominantly Christian also. We shall quote from C. S. Braden's book *These Also Believe: A Study of Modern American Cults and Minority Religious Movements* (New York, Macmillan, 1949). Of course you may not accept some or any of their doctrines. But their existence is evidence that many have been deeply concerned to help their fellows here and now, feeling as they do that the churches haven't done enough. It was the love-urge that originated these increasing sects. The older denominations may look askance at them because of differences in their doctrines, and thereby fail to see the significance of their arrival. That significance lies in the witness of a great upsurge of the love-gospel, greater than ever in the past

New Sects

We select some of them to show their sincere love-motive, love applied, we might call it. Hear for instance what is taught by the sect *Psychiana*. "You may learn to use this fathomless, pulsing, throbbing ocean of spiritual power just as you learn to use chemistry, physics, or mathematics" (p. 83). "You may find the power of God and actually use it to bring to you and yours, *while you are alive,* a superabundance of happiness, peace, comfort, financial security, domestic happiness—in fact, everything for your own good. Now. . ." (p. 83). Note the emphasis on bettering the everyday life for all. Then there is the New Thought group, declaring "the immediate availability of God. . .practical application of spiritual thought-force to the solution of human problems" (p. 129). It has produced the International New Thought Alliance. It "influences fifteen to twenty million people in America" (p. 130). In the same direction is Christian Science, spreading as it has done to England, the continent of Europe, South Africa, Australia, South America (p. 136). This sect agrees with the teaching of that wonderful Negro Father Divine in worshipping the Father-Mother God—a recognition not given in the past Protestant sects to the feminine element in the good life. Our author avows of the New Thought that "together with Christian Science, it constitutes a spiritual movement as significant for our day as the Reformation was for its time" (p. 130). Perhaps the most remarkable of these sects, for the onlooking outsider, is Unity. This body, we are told, didn't intend to be a sect, but gradually became one. (Human nature loves to be in a single group—this and no other!) ". . .they discourage people from leaving other churches to come into their own" (p. 147). Their influence seems to be strong: "thousands of letters, telegrams, and telephone calls. . . from all over the United States and even from foreign lands, requesting help through prayer" (p. 148). Surely the love-motive is evident here, even if you think it misdirected; the name *Unity* signifies it. This group, we are told, came out of Christian Science, but is closer to the New Thought, and is "the largest and strongest numerically and institutionally of any of the New Thought groups" (p. 156). All of the above sects center on this earthly life: "regeneration of the body" (p. 160). For

Unity "it is eternal life in the body which is the desired goal" (p. 164). And hear this: "man must cultivate love until it becomes the keynote of his life" (p. 165); must have "religion as a constant factor in life, not merely occasional" (put off to Sunday!) (p. 177). Unity indeed is a very impressive movement: "The total investment in plant, farm, and Unity Centers, now runs into millions of dollars" (p. 177). And speaking of the emergence of the feminine in modern times, it is notable too that "In the newer religious movements in America women have played a much more important role than in the older groups" (p. 221). Beside the above named sects are Spiritualism, Theosophy, the *I am* sect. Here women have played a strong part: the Fox sisters, Edna Ballard, Amy Mcpherson, Helen Blavatsky, Annie Besant. And most spiritualist mediums have been women. If man, as Aristotle said, is the political animal, many have also discerned that woman is the religious animal. Into the doctrines of these more esoteric sects we needn't go: the point is, they illustrate the same forward surge of the love-motive as do the others. All are deeply concerned with a fuller, better, happier life for their fellow men and women here and now on earth. When the religious motive is directed chiefly to a blessed future life in the spirit, it is more likely to be self-centered; so it has been in the past with many of the Christian churches—join the church and you'll be saved. But when religion turns more toward the matters of earthly life, it becomes more of a working attitude, practical here and now. As said above, the modern "social gospel" so emphasized in recent years is an emergence of the love-urge not before seen. And the notable thing about these new sects is just that emergence: life here and now for God's children all over the world must be enlarged, bettered, purified, prolonged. Some of the sects teach that we shall finally overcome death itself. "The last great enemy that shall be destroyed is death" says the Revelation of St. John.

We but note one more of the new sects, Jehovah's Witnesses. True, it declares itself, we are told, to be 5000 years old, but it didn't become a recognized sect until 1872. We mention here but one point: it predicts "The Kingdom of Heaven is at hand. The end of the age is near. Armageddon is just around the corner, when the wicked will be destroyed and the Theocracy, or rule of God, will be set up on earth. Be warned!" (p. 370). And "salvation is to be experienced rather on earth" not an "escape from earth to another life" (p. 378). If the love-motive is not quite so outstanding here—this sect condemns the other religious groups, quite in the opposite spirit to that of Unity—yet the stress upon the life here in the flesh, the practical motive of the love-urge, is evident.

We needn't notice the many other sects. Enough to see that what stirs these earnest ones to start some new movement is their feeling of the failure of the older churches to have made mankind better. They are saddened by the spectacle, they love their fellows, they *must* discover some new way out. No matter how wrong you may believe their creeds, no matter how misdirected you may conceive their methods, there can be no doubt that they are led by a deep sympathy with the sufferings of their fellows and a devoted effort to lighten and brighten their life on earth. See also that many of the sects, trying as they are to better mankind's earthly life, are using their intelligence more than was done in the older churches on the whole. Note the titles: New *Thought,* Christian *Science*. These sects don't rely *exclusively* on some Divine revelation. They try to reason out a systematic theology, more or less. They don't declare "believe or go to hell", they plead to us to consider their new teaching and see if it isn't well-grounded, reasonable. Modern love in Christianity seems to have more of deliberate thoughtful choice than was the case before.

But beside this increasing respect for thought, there is a

specially outstanding factor in a number of these new sects—
a factor which has also stood out strong in some of the older
sects, as we have noted earlier. New Thought, Christian Science, Theosophy, and Spiritualism have shown it markedly. It
is the *practical* demonstration of the power of spirit over the
flesh now and here, a power available to all who will try it
to cure disease. Of course, the thing is old. At first it was a
belief in magic, and no doubt it worked successfully now and
then. It has lasted in one form or another through the centuries, and above all in Christianity. The miracles of Jesus
have given it a basis in religion. And He said: "The things
that I do ye shall do, and more also." But it has been brought
into the highlight especially by the sects just named. Long
latent in Christian teaching, it is now out in the open. And
see what this means. It means that the spirit-world is coming
closer to the material arena where lives mankind. No longer
is that world *only* something to look forward to after you die.
It is that, of course, but it now heralds the presence of spiritual
forces in *this* world. The love-motive has grown greater, more
inclusive.

To look back on all the examples so far: the simple fact,
confirmed by plain observation of what people *do,* not what
they answer to questionnaires, is that today, and especially in
the U. S. A., we have a spirit of consideration for the needs
of others such as was never so widespread in the past. This
spirit is love; it is nothing else. It may be misdirected, perhaps
it is bound to be so until it is filled out with much reflection
and experience. But the love-motive is there, the necessary
and in the end the sufficient condition of its own right direction. And perhaps the most striking thing about it is this:
whereas in the past the kindly deeds were mostly by individuals alone, nowadays they are so largely by groups, whose
members are in loving agreement with one another, helping
one another in the good work.

Now for the organized love-work of the Christian churches as a clear-cut element in their religion: the Christian foreign missions. Not many of the laity have any idea of the extent of their deeds, of their practical effect in helping the living conditions of the people for whom they work. We dwell on these missions particularly because they show so well the *breadth* of Christian love, extending beyond their own relatives, friends, fellow-citizens, to mankind at large. In the other nations there is perhaps more, perhaps less, of this widely diffused love, enough to stress what is happening in this large and strong nation, the U. S. A.

Catholic Missions

To see the prodigious reach of our foreign missions, begin with the work of the Roman Catholic Church, which sends its missionaries all over the world. We start with this because its record is so stupendous, so much so that we cannot go very far into detail. We quote first from the booklet *U. S. Catholic Overseas Missionary Personnel* of January 1, 1956, published by the Mission Secretariat, Washington, D. C. For further information consult also the journal *Missions,* Bishop Fulton J. Sheen, Editor, October 1957. (What we are here saying was written early in 1958.) Note that our topic is foreign missions, no interest just now in work done to help the needy in the U. S. A.

In the *Introduction* by Bishop Sheen we read of "the 134 religious (Catholic) institutes who send missionaries outside the United States" (p. 6). And "no other country in the world gives so much to the support of its missions as does the United States. . . . The American people give much, not because they have much—for the missions have been, and will always be supported by those who have relatively little—but rather because they love much the missions of the Church . . . . How many missionaries does the United States presently have serving outside of its boundaries? 5,126. . . . This is the first time in the history of the Church in the United States that the number has ever exceeded five thousand" (p. 6). By the way, it is impressive to notice before giving numbers concerning overseas missions in different regions, that the missions serving within the U. S. A. only, contain 48,439 priests; 161,741 sisters, and 8,868 brothers. See table, p. 7., and mark the greater number of sisters! Typically, hasn't woman more love in her make-up than man?

To go on, "Out of a total of 5,126 priests, brothers and sisters, 1,944 . . . serve in Latin America . . . 1,184 are serving in the vast non-Christian area of Asia. Japan and Korea register good gains during the past two years. Americans in Japan have increased from 247 to 312 and those in Korea from 39 to 68. . . . American missionaries among the Chinese (that is in Formosa, Hong Kong and Macao) have decreased to 234 from the 334 reported two years ago" (p. 9). Due to Communism, no doubt.

"Africa has a small population in relation to its area, but is the most important continent for the future of the world. . . . The total number of missionaries in Africa serving under the Propaganda is 30,595 of which number only 445 are from the United States" (p. 9). "In relation to the population, Oceania seems to have a great appeal to the missionaries of the United States. 764 United States Priests, Brothers and Sisters evangelize in Oceania, which represents 15% of our total overseas personnel (p. 10). . . . The remaining 6.3% of the United States mission body is stationed in the Arctic, in mission posts in Australia and New Zealand. . . . It is encouraging to report that religious institutes in general are sending more personnel to missions outside of the United States. . . . Men's institutes total 54, while women's institutes total 80, a grand total of 134 United States religious bodies with members overseas. A number of additional institutes appear in this year's brochure because, even though they have no United States members overseas as yet, they report mission candidates in training.

"Of the 54 sending societies representing Priests and Brothers, 33 report an aggregate increase overseas in these two years (1954-6) of 272. Eight societies report no change in their total. Thirteen societies report a decrease of an aggregate of 129, principally in the China area. (Due to Communism, of course!) Thus the net increase of missionary Priests and Brothers has been 143 (p. 10).

"Of the 80 sending societies of women, 38 report an increase in total members overseas for an aggregate of 301. No change in totals overseas has been experienced by 24 societies. A decrease in the overseas total is reported by 18 societies for an aggregate loss of 73. Thus the net gain in members overseas for the 80 societies is 228 (p. 11).

"Building hospitals, clinics, and dispensaries that would have frightened into lethargy women of other generations, the American nun takes in her stride" (p. 13).

Note the increase in numbers from 1940 on. Over Africa as a whole the increase goes from 108 in 1940 to 445 in 1956; in Asia for the same dates from 1305 to 1658, in Oceania from 229 to 809; in Europe from 20 to 102; in Middle America (we here omit the U. S. A. and Canada) from 68 to 329; in West Indies from 267 to 887; in South America from 154 to 728. See then the practical work—showing the true love-motive more than ever.

Into the details of the various institutes—of men 54 in the U. S. A., of women 80, as noted, we need not go. The work they do, in addition to conversion, is indicated as we go through the list from p. 16 to p. 61: "Education", "clinics", "social work", "medicine", "works of mercy", "charitable work", "care of the sick", "maintain hospitals and leprosaria", "direct printing houses", "care of orphanages", "industrial training", "establishment of cooperatives", "training of lay teachers", "vocational training", "charitable houses", "nursing", "conduct of a general hospital and a nursing home", "child welfare work", "maternity cases", "train native nurses", "maintain grade and high schools", "social activities among the very poor", "maintenance of houses of refuge". And all this the world over.

To add some facts, we quote in part from tables furnished by the Catholic Mission Society of Hartford Diocese— kindness of Rt. Rev. Joseph M. Griffin. These apply to the United States, Alaska, Juneau and Honolulu in 1956. General Hospitals 795. Bed capacity in General Hospitals, 127,681. Homes for the Aged, 302. Special Hospitals or Sanatoria, 136. Bed capacity in Special Hospitals 10,666. Schools for Nurses, 341. Orphanages and Infant Asylums, 317. Children in Orphanages and Asylums, 34,346. Children cared for in Foster Homes, 22,088. Student Nurses, 35,267. Inmates in Homes for the Aged, 26,827. The following figures "concern only the territories dependent on the S. Congregation De Propaganda Fide." Teachers in Asia, 44,648; in Africa, 80,127; in Oceania, 11,699. Medical Doctors in Asia, 239; in Africa, 161; in Oceania, 31. Nurses in Asia, 1446; in Africa, 2,232; in Oceania, 914. Enrollment in Elementary Schools in Asia, 748,740; in Africa, 3,114,946; in Oceania, 368,118. Enrollment in Secondary Schools in Asia, 627,194; in Africa, 231,-151; in Oceania, 220,041. In Professional Schools and Colleges in Asia, 19,956; in Africa, 53,541; in Oceania, 19,058. Orphans in Orphanages in Asia, 63,474; in Africa, 22,992; in Oceania, 12,458. Inmates in Homes for the Aged in Asia, 5,021; in Africa, 3,501; in Oceania, 2,457. Beds in Hospitals in Asia, 13,400; in Africa, 38,226; in Oceania, 11,102. Patients of Dispensaries in Asia, 8,968,965; in Africa, 42,117,-700; in Oceania, 4,898,399. Lepers in Leprosaria in Asia, 4,430; in Africa, 48,807; in Oceania, 1,335. "These statistics did not cover Red China, North Korea, Vietnam, Laos, and Cambodia." In Canada, "Works of charity were carried out in 259 hospitals and clinics, besides 249 orphanages, asylums and other protective institutions." In the Bahamas in 1956 were 74 lay teachers, 1 physician, 12 kindergartens, 1 nursery, 3 maternity clinics. In Java, 7 missionary territories; in Sumatra 5; in Borneo-Celebes 9; in Formosa 5. In "Territories in America dependent on the Congregation De Propaganda Fide" there were in 1956: Teachers 5,711; Medical Doctors 24; Nurses 431; Orphans in Orphanages 8,348; Inmates of Homes for the Aged 1,156; Beds in Hospitals 6,738; Patients of Dispensaries 657,235; Lepers in Leprosaria 900.

We would here emphasize the fact that while conversion to Christianity is everywhere and always the end in view, the *way* of conversion is the way of love. The missions work to better the lives of the men, the women, the children, in every possible way *in this world*. They *love* those they work for, love them as individuals who should live happily and fruitfully. Nothing of the bad old way of some past Christians: "turn Christian or go to hell!" Rather it is, "join with us in the life of love for all," and showing that love by concrete helpful deeds.

See now the work performed by the Protestant Christian missions the world over, work infused, like the above, with a loving effort to better the condition of the less advanced peoples. The information here is furnished by the Rev. Henry van Dusen who has, we believe, done more than any one else to reveal the extent of this work.

Protestant Missions

These missions have labored and today are laboring more than ever in the following areas: China, Japan, India, Indonesia, Dutch East Indies, Philippines, Belgian Congo, Korea, Africa's Gold Coast, Formosa, Central Africa, Cameroun, Liberia, Thailand—in the larger countries, of course, more missions than in the smaller.

Read the account in Dr. van Dusen's book, *For the Healing of the Nations* (New York, Scribners, 1943), telling of his journey around the world to visit as many missions as time would permit before attending the Madras Conference. This is then an account by a direct witness. It opens with his visit to Celebes, island of the Dutch East Indies. Attention in what follows is not so much centered on the U. S. A. missions as was the case with the Catholic missions. Consider a characteristic example. He writes, ". . . we entered a typical village . . . to the left, a brown steeple lifted above the trees revealing a little Dutch church. Beyond, a plain square building unmistakably announced the village school. A little farther on and across the road, a low, one-storied white building suggested a hospital (pp. 19-20). . . . Both of our hosts had been leaders of the Dutch Student Christian Movement in undergraduate days. After medical course and internship in Holland and a couple of years of special preparation in tropical diseases in Java, he had come here as his first appointment. Before her marriage, she was a full graduate in theology at the University of Utrecht," (p. 20). "We met the head of the school-system for that locality with responsibility for some sixty-five schools scattered through the mountains. Also the 'language expert'— a brilliant linguist who is giving his life to the mastery of the native dialects in order that a door may be opened for these primitive peoples to the riches of mankind's learning and literature. The doctor inquired if we cared to see the leper sanitarium. . . . A dozen little homes, beautifully designed and constructed by local workmanship . . . and tastefully decorated by the lepers themselves, housed a hundred and ten lepers. . . . We passed in and out among the residents. On one porch a leprous mother rocked a newborn infant. Before another, children played in the sand. Everywhere cheerful contented faces and cordial greetings welcomed us. We learned that the less severe cases can be cured. 'But,' I said, 'there are no walls, no fences, no guards.' The doctor smiled, 'Of course not. No one wants to leave,' (p. 22). . . . "It was late evening before we found time to visit the hospital itself . . . seventy beds always overcrowded. For the constituency of that little hospital numbers 300,000 people. And the area of responsibility is close to 10,000 square miles of jagged mountains pierced by hardly a road. It must be covered mainly on horseback, visiting a dozen dispensaries which supplement the work of the central hospital. The medical staff consists of one doctor and one trained nurse, assisted by locally trained native helpers. Tuberculosis, venereal disease, leprosy, cholera, trachoma, rupture—these are the major ailments. At the moment the most crying need is an electric plant, but that is a dream to conjure with for the future. When I was saying good night and laid on the table a small bill—less than an evening's theater at home —the young doctor grasped my hand with tears in his eyes. As we drove off in the gray dawn the following morning (p. 23) our last glimpse . . . was of two dim figures standing in the doorway where they had greeted us on the previous day —weary and a little haggard, but still smiling. General practitioner, surgeon, obstetrician, ophthalmologist, orthopedist, tropical disease specialist, leprosy expert, friend-at-large to 300,000 primitive people!

"This incident . . . the human situation disclosed and the work of the Christian Church toward meeting that need—it could be multiplied many times from our very limited observations in this small corner of the world. The islands of the Netherlands Indies alone—60,000,000 people, half the population of the United States, vast numbers of them entirely without medicine, without education, without faith save for the work of the little Christian churches" (p. 24). If you want more examples like the above, read the rest of this impressive book! But let us add two more quotations.

"The typical Christian mission is not a church (or the shade of a palm tree as improvised substitute) in which a solitary preacher exhorts simple native folk to turn from their habitual superstitions and rites to worship the Christian God . . . the typical mission is a center of three or four buildings—hospital, school, church—from which a team of co-workers . . . minister, doctor, teacher, nurse, social worker, agriculturalist go forth . . . to all who will accept their help" (p. 174).

And this: "Dr.———(we omit names), a Canadian medical missionary of thirty-eight whose station had fallen into the hands of the Japanese, had gone west before their advance into so-called 'Red China'. For five months he had been circling the provinces of Shensi and Shansa, traversing a thousand miles almost altogether on foot. In the last six weeks, he had walked twenty to forty miles each day, treating soldiers whose wounds had gone as long as three years without attention, from daylight to dusk, day after day administering medical relief to all sorts and conditions of folk from the foremost leaders of 'Communist China' to the humblest peasants, soldiers and civilians, Chinese and Japanese, without discrimination" (p. 64). The doctor himself said, as quoted by the writer: "In one district alone within a radius of three miles were 1400 wounded and sick—no doctors, no supplies" (p. 64). And "It was trying to awake every morning with the sick and wounded pulling at your bedclothes, but you get used to it" (pp. 64-65). We add the following from data furnished by Dr. van Dusen in an unpublished list.

In the Belgian Congo are 35 leper colonies, ministering to some 6000 patients; 171 Christian hospitals, 200 missionary doctors, 1000 African assistants; 12,000 schools, 400,000 pupils, 1700 missionaries. As quoted from a captain in the

United States Army Medical Corps, "Thirty-five thousand patients were treated here last year . . . it is inspiring to see what these missionaries do and how they are beloved and respected by the natives." In Lucknow there is the Isabella Thorburn College for women—only a single illustration of what is being done for the emancipation of women in India. In Africa south of the Sahara, 85% of all school education is due to missionaries. In the Gold Coast there are 2500 new schools. In Formosa there are 100 new churches. "In the Christian World Missions, denominational differences are largely accidental and irrelevant. . . . No other movement in human history has ever spread so rapidly and widely in so brief a period of time."

We have been treating of Protestant missions in general. Among the Protestants are the Quakers, much of whose work has been included in the above. Yet the deeds of the Quakers are so outstanding as to deserve special emphasis.

Work Of The Quakers

One of their highly esteemed leaders, Rufus M. Jones, in *A Call to What is Vital* (New York, Macmillan, 1948) says of them: "They have rebuilt and reorganized the villages of the Marne Valley in France which the first World War destroyed. They have rebuilt the villages of the Verdun Department of France which the war left totally scorched and wrecked. They have brought cows into Vienna when there was no milk in this great city; they also brought in coal from Hungary in their Ford cars and kept the hospital fires going, and they stayed and helped the people of Vienna through three disastrous revolutions. They went to Germany in 1920 and for four years they fed and nourished the children who were starved by the blockade which was carried on to force Germany to sign the peace treaty. At the peak of this service of love they fed more than a million children a day.

They sent a tractor unit to Poland to help the refugees—who were returning from Russia—to plow their long neglected fields, and they stayed, at the cost of their lives, to help fight the typhus epidemic which swept over Poland after the close of the war. . . . During and since the end of World War II the English, American and Canadian Quakers have carried on an almost world-wide work of relief. The ambulance work and trucking system in West China, especially on the Burma Road, and the work of relief during the disastrous famine in Bengal in India, are two of the most impressive undertakings" (pp. 130-131). He adds on p. 132: "Meantime, in our neighboring land of Mexico, the Quakers have helped to rebuild a region levelled by earthquake. They have drained swamps in the fight against malaria. They have built schoolhouses and playgrounds, and they have taught the children games and how to care for their bodies. All this work in all these countries that sounds secular has been penetrated and infused with a spirit of love. . . *though there has been no attempt to win adherents to the Quaker Society,*" (italics added). This last clause is refutation enough of the cynical objection that all these good Christians are only trying to convert the world and thereby gain a world-power, even as the Communists are trying to do today.

In the *American Friends Service Committee Bulletin,* May-June 1957, there is this on the cover: "Let us then try what love will do . . . to Relieve Suffering . . . to build Peace . . . to Strengthen Community." This journal records the work done by the Committee since its formation in 1917, giving details with dates. These we cannot here go into, but anyone who worries over the problems of our time should read thoroughly this issue of the *Bulletin.* The A. F. S. C. must surely have done notable things, for it was awarded the Nobel Prize in 1947. The whole account breathes the spirit of love through and through. What needs stressing is the maximum of *practi-*

cal deeds, feeding children and the like, and particularly the *spirit* in which they are done. Above all and through all have they sought to infuse the love-motive in those whom they help, to abolish strife and hatred. Nor do they believe this to be an easy task: "the starving child can always be fed, but when one comes to deal with the more subtle things that engender ill-will and hatred between races and nations, one is confronted with a far more difficult task." And, "the A. F. S. C. has always been more concerned with prevention than with picking up the pieces, with reconciliation more than with relief for its own sake."

Remember that these "conscientious objectors" have made up for their refusal to fight by active work to help the wounded, and such.

Let us add to this account of the Friends' work by quoting from page 11 of the *Bulletin,* the "Six Months Report of Material Aids and Shipments", (October 1, 1956 to April 1, 1957). Clothing, shoes, bedding, textiles, soap, drugs, and the like: "400,000 pounds to Austria for the relief of Hungarians, 612,000 pounds to Cuba, Egypt, France, Germany, Italy, Japan, Korea, Jordan, U. S. A. Government surplus and other food: 304,000 pounds to Austria for the relief of Hungarians, 3,946,000 pounds to Germany, Hungary, Italy, Japan, Korea—5,262,000 pounds total shipments."

And finally you should look at the Report for the year 1962 by the A. F. S. C. which tells of what the Quakers are doing in Africa among the 29 small newly independent nations which have emerged since 1950, all too weak, ignorant, poor, and ridden with disease. The work these good Quakers have been doing to overcome these grave troubles by education, poor relief, medication, building villages, and such is just tremendous. Above all, they are stressing in their work the spirit of peaceful cooperation, a motive greatly needed by these newborn nations with their fighting between and within themselves, hardly fit to be nations as yet.

So much then for the labors of these good Christians, work whose vast extent is seldom realized by those who look at the overall world scene today with its public fights.

But there is also at hand a further ground for hope, one which hasn't been noticed much by the religious ones. There is a hint, even a probability, of our making our earthly life more and more infused with the spiritual. And this evidence has hardly been stressed by our physical scientists—it makes no big headlines in newspapers or journals.

It is as if spirit-powers are descending gradually more and more into our bodily life, our separation from one another in space, from the future in time.

Recent Psychical Research

Look at the results of "psychical research" as it is called. We cannot reasonably doubt that it has proved the existence of telepathy, clairvoyance, precognition, telekinesis. These experiences are to a high degree, if not wholly, independent of space and time. They are directly aware of distant events, distant in space and time, with no such physical stimulus from the object as occurs in everyday seeing, hearing, or other sensing. In telekinesis they are *producing* such events. They are *purely* spiritual affairs. Yet they occur to us, located as we are in our bodies. The point is not so much that they are new, probably they have been present in mankind for centuries. But of late we have become increasingly aware of their presence and their power. The spirit-realm is emerging into the light of common day. We see the *exclusions* of space and time to a high degree overcome. We receive messages from our distant loved ones. Not that these "supernormal" experiences lead necessarily to good deeds, to more love for our fellows. But they do open the door wider to a region where our powers, rightly used, *may* possibly bring about many goods to our fellows which on a merely physical plane we couldn't give them. At any rate, the spirit-realm is coming to the forefront more and more. Isn't it almost as if we are discovering a new continent? Look also at the claims of the mediums, as well as of many private individuals, that they have received messages from friends who have survived death. The parapsychologists, as they are called, investigating with rigidly controlled scientific method, are not yet ready to say these are proved. But the fact is, such experiences, be they delusions or not, are now coming more and more to the front. And also, whether delusions or not, they do seem to be motivated so often by the *loving* departed ones. See the book by Gardner Murphy, *Challenge of Psychical Research* (New York, Harpers, 1961). More directly in line with the love-motive, however, are the growing numbers of so-called faith cures. Not only the sect of Christian Scientists and other groups of "New Thought", but the very numerous healings by men such as Oral Roberts and T. L. Osborn, here in the U. S. A. and also abroad as in Africa—all these point to a strong upsurge of spirit-forces here and now in our physical bodies. So far, and quite far it is too, are the limitations, the evils due to the conflicts between the urge to live and the physical forces of nature, being overcome, and by the love-urge to help all mankind.

Look back now over the evidence we have given of the growing Christian love today. In the words of Arnold Toynbee "Our world has risen to an unprecedented degree of humanitarian feeling" (*Civilization on Trial,* New York, Oxford University Press, 1948, p. 150). And such feeling is the love-urge, the help-one-another motive. As we said, there is but one kind of love. If as we Christians believe, God is love, this growing love in our human hearts and deeds is the Divine love entering therein. Many who don't admit the supernatural would not acknowledge this; but it is the fact, *if* the Divine Lover is really implied in that striving for the good which is inevitable in all of us, know it or not. And this is borne out by what the above evidence shows. The love-motive, we saw, has spread itself greatly of late; yet it has penetrated, on the whole, more deeply within in the case of those who worship the Supreme Lover. Certainly on the whole, by and large the world over, the Christian peoples have contributed more in works of love as seen in the immense number of their charities, organized and individual, and the practical ministrations of the Christian missions. There is the pragmatic justifying we spoke of: the supernatural virtue of love has given and is more and more giving a depth, an intensity, to a here-and-now better life. Even the materialist and "humanist", as we said, are feeling the love-motive as never before. And now that our Christian churches are laying more stress on mankind's social relations, there is surely less personal hostility between them than there used to be. Here read the book *Liberal Theology, an Appraisal* (New York, Charles Scribner's Sons, 1942), a symposium which helps to confirm our thesis. Also, as we said, the greater our fear of an all-destroying war the nearer we come to feeling the need of a world-over loving harmony of the nations. Yes, whatever our evils, there is so far a greater ground for hope than in the old days when we didn't dread destructive wars.

And surely all the empirical evidence we have given does have a result of the utmost significance: it has *verified* the law of the three stages, it has shown that law *at work*. Isn't it then as much a law as the physical laws of gravitation, electric attraction, and such? If it is, it *must* be fulfilled, mustn't it?

Really, the whole weight of the evidence turns on this: those who would deny its claim do so because their attention has been centered *only* on the present evils. They haven't thought of comparing what we are feeling and doing today with what in the past was felt and done by mankind for long centuries. They don't see the great progress we have made beyond those old cruelties, hatred of one another as they were, nothing to compare with the compassion so many feel today, realizing our human pains as they were never realized for ages, scarcely felt at all except by the saints and prophets, so few and far between. How long it was before the great religions came forth! Even one of the earliest, Vedanta, with its search for a heavenly bliss, didn't concern itself at all with the lower grade, the "untouchables". Not until about 500 B. C. did the love-motive blossom strong in the Eastern religions, as with Gautama the Buddha. In the light of history the love-religions came only after long ages. No, the lack of conviction by the evidence here given lies in the doubter's failing to sense the great progress achieved from primitive man's cruelties, ignorance, pains, prolonged indeed even to mediaeval times.

Come then to the second theme of our argument, concerned with the very grave evils in our world today.

Evidence As To Present Evils

You may say that our evidence of the increased and increasing love-motive has been drawn from just one nation, the U. S. A. How about the people of the Middle East, the Far East, of Africa—witness the Congolese today—of the Pacific islands, of South America? How about fighting Red China? Clearly the evils in these have increased, more conflicts within and between them than ever before. And they cover a much larger part of the world than does the U. S. A., a far greater number of suffering human beings with their overpopulation and sickness, their newly originated nations fighting or aiding Communism, adding to our human warfare. Isn't there then much more evil today than ever before?

But now see this. These evils are of two sorts: *individual* personal suffering and fighting between *groups, nations.* As to the first, even if we have centered our attention on our corner of the world, we have seen how much we have lessened the sufferings of many many individuals by our missionary work the world over. It doesn't matter who did this, the point is that it has been done, and has actually helped far more individual sufferers than was done in the past. How few of the deniers of our claim have considered this evidence! Nor is the work confined as much as they would say to our corner of the world. For instance, the social gospel has permeated India of late—a big step away from the old exclusions of caste. Think of Gandhi, think of the work of Albert Schweitzer in Africa. And monogamy with its increasing respect for woman's rights is now seeping into Islam. No, it is not the sufferings, sickness, ignorance of individuals as just in themselves which have increased. It is rather that in modern days we have come to realize their extent as never in the past. And that realization has lessened them the world over.

Yes, it is the social conflicts, the struggles between the groups, the nations, wars, hot and cold, increasing crimes, it is *these* evils which stand out so clearly as having grown wider and more intense today. So now take a look at them.

The Increasing Conflicts Of Groups

Of late years as never before there came on the scene a struggle by one nation to dominate the world. The Nazis— as we said above—deeming themselves the one group better in every way, superior to all others, would do that. So came the two WORLD wars, extending to the West and to the Far East. Fortunately for mankind, they were defeated. Then another nation sought world-domination, not now deeming its peoples a superior race, but believing its social scheme the best possible for all mankind. There was in the U. S. S. R. more of an extension beyond the power-motive than in the Nazis. They followed an ideal social system, *thought* out by Karl Marx—the intelligence-motive now at work. And there was also the dawning love-motive, as we noted above, their belief that their system would benefit all mankind. Yet they did retain the old power-motive; they would *force* their citizens to accept the system, no falling away permitted, and they would if opposed by other nations fight those nations. But very fortunately again, had come the discovery of the deadly atom bomb—a power able to destroy their own nation well-nigh at once, as well as their opposing nations. The situation was critical, a crisis such as never before had occurred in history. They couldn't convince their opponents of their system, they *must* somehow dominate the world, they would *have* to do it by force, wouldn't they? But if they started a war, those deadly weapons would be just as likely to blot out *their* nation as to obliterate their enemies. It is gradually becoming clearer that they don't want another world war any more than we do. The plain fact is that the increasing conflicts are due to the smaller groups, nations, especially in the East and in Africa. When the Communist seeks to convert them, some welcome his system, some oppose it, warfare comes in within this or that group. Witness the scene in Southeast Asia! Even without open declaration of war, guerilla warfare goes on. These smaller groups haven't been impressed, as have the larger nations, with the dread of total destruction by the atomic weapons. And why not? They haven't enough of the scientific outlook to be so deeply impressed. They are as compared with Russia and the U. S. A., backward, undeveloped. They haven't gone very far in the second stage of the above law, the stage of intellect, seen in the development of the sciences.

Particularly is this the case with the young small nations

recently released from the colonial status—e. g. Ghana and
others in Africa and the East. Note by the way that this re-
leasing, this gift of independence by the greater nations who
owned them, is itself a case of the increasing love-motive in
those greater nations. They wanted the colonies to be free to
develop themselves, to realize their own possible goods by their
own work. So England liberated India, the U. S. A. freed the
Philippines, and the like with Holland and others. Yet the
liberated ones haven't responded very much to this kindness.
Even though the strong nations have contributed much to
those whom they released—gifts of money, machines, schools
—the young nations have shown little gratitude, rather have
they expressed resentment, dislike, even hostility. For one
instance, though not a case of colonial release, which examples
this attitude, how have some of them responded to the vast
amounts of money, schools, hospitals and such given by the
U. S. A.? They have come to express more and more their
dislike of this nation; they are openly jealous of it with its
power and high standards of living. And why? Because of
their own weakness! These newly born little nations are, in
the national arena, in the childhood stage. As we saw above,
this stage is the first of the three given by the *law*. It is the
power-seeking stage. As the child would increase his strength
by his efforts, so the newly born young nation would increase
its strength, not just by being helped from without but by its
own independent effort. And surely that is *so far* right! The
greater and richer nations of today went through that same
stage in their youth.

Yes, these young nations resent the implication of superiori-
ty in the nations which are helping them. They want to be
strong just of themselves, independent of help from superiors.
They are in the first of the three stages of the law, the power
stage. And as the greater nations of today grew from that
stage to the second, with their growing intelligence leading

to greater prosperity, and are now to a degree entering the third stage, with their longing for world-peace, we cannot but expect that these young nations will do the like—all the more because the world is now more closely knit than in the past. Our interest in science and intelligence will the more easily come to permeate their outlook, and as they grow more reflective they will come to realize more and more the need of world-peace.

Of course there remains still the great fight between Communism and Democracy, leading as it does so much to the conflicts between and within these smaller groups. Yet the prospect here is better than it looks on the surface. As we noted, Russia of late has been less filled with the fighting spirit—Khrushchev was less of a fighter than Stalin. Recall the test-ban. Also notice the recent passage allowed from East to West Berlin. It is not so much in Russia as in the later convert to Communism, Red China, that the fighting spirit is strong. Red China is contributing more than Russia to the conflicts in the smaller nations—witness what is happening in Southeast Asia.

But see now what has taken place within these two large nations which are trying out the Communist plan. The experiment isn't succeeding very well! We saw in Chapter I that the right thing to do with a social scheme is to test it, carry it out, live it in the group which believes in it. See if it works! That is the truly scientific method. Well, Russia and Red China have rightly been doing this, and it has brought about more suffering in their nations than before. The food supply has diminished much. And the like has come about in Cuba, recent Western convert to their scheme. Discontent among the peoples of these nations has increased. The kinder nations—England, U. S. A.—have even tried to help them by trading with them, supplying wheat and other sources of needed food. The Communist plan is failing! Of course the reason is obvious; it suppresses individual initiative. They don't, for instance, permit the farmer to think out new ways of improving his work, to help himself and his family. They haven't realized that all human advance, new and better ways of living, originates in the mind of the individual. The individual must think for himself! True indeed, the danger has usually been that he will think *only* for his own good, not for that of his fellows also. In the Democratic society which permits much freedom to the individual, that danger has in the past—as Karl Marx and his followers have seen—led to many instances where the individual has sought only his own and his family's wealth, or that of his small group, giving those who work under him scant wages, oppressing the poor, the laboring class—the essential evil as the Marxists say, of what they dub Capitalism. Yet as a plain fact, this particular evil has practically vanished in the present Democratic society, owing to the freedom granted to labor, seen in its frequent strikes. No, it certainly looks as if the Communist scheme couldn't succeed in the end, it is being *shown* by its experiment, its scientific method, to intelligence witnessing what occurs. There is the ground for expecting the second stage, intelligence, to round out eventually in the third stage which with its love-motive respects *both* the interests of the nation as a whole *and* the value of the individual initiative just in itself.

Yes, this empirical evidence does help to confirm the law of the three stages. The new, small nations are in the first stage, and as they become more educated, more thoughtful about the consequences of the bitter fights, they must sooner or later come to see and feel the demand for world-peace. And the increasingly evident failure of the Communist scheme with its exclusion of individual initiative must sooner or later lead its defenders to admit and respect that indispensable good—thereby increasing the love-motive, the third stage. In short, to stress it once more, it is the law of the three stages, not yet seen by those who look at the surface of things today, which justifies that brighter outlook brought to light when we reviewed above the progress of mankind through the centuries. Above all, as we have said, the deeper confirmation of this law lies in this: it is the temporal expression of the nature of the Creator, as seen in His Triune being: Power the First Person, Reason, logos the Second, Love the Third, the Holy Spirit. The effect *must* in the end express in its analogous and finite way, the nature of the Cause. As our intelligence develops into the love-stage, our free choices, hitherto between the good and the evil, will be exercised more and more between goods that don't conflict.

No, as we take a long and broad survey of the human situation, past and present, and thereby bring to light the working, however slowly, of the *Law of the Three Stages,* the evidence does look to justify a far brighter prospect for the future than can be discerned by those who look only at our present evils.